BEAD IT, IRON IT, LOVE IT!

BEAD IT, IRON IT, LOVE IT!
OVER 300 GREAT MOTIFS FOR FUSE BEADS

Kaisa Holsting

BARRON'S

A QUARTO BOOK

First edition for the United States and
Canada published in 2015 by Barron's
Educational Series, Inc.

All inquiries should be addressed to:
Barron's Educational Series, Inc.
250 Wireless Boulevard
Hauppauge, NY 11788
www.barronseduc.com

ISBN: 978-1-4380-0753-3
Library of Congress Control No:
2015948241

Conceived, designed, and produced by
Quarto Publishing plc
The Old Brewery
6 Blundell Street
London, N7 9BH

QUAR. BILO

Senior project editor: Chelsea Edwards
Senior art editor: Emma Clayton
Designer: Joanna Bettles
Photographers: Phil Wilkins and
Simon Pask
Illustrators: Iriini Kalliomäki and
John Woodcock
Copy editor: Claire Waite Brown
Proofreader: Emma Hill
Indexer: Helen Snaith
Art director: Caroline Guest
Creative director: Moira Clinch
Publisher: Paul Carslake

Color separation in Singapore by Pica
Digital Pte Limited
Printed in China by 1010 Printing
International Limited
9 8 7 6 5 4 3 2 1

FOR THE LOVE OF PIXELS!

My love affair with fuse beads started when I was 12 years old and I got a fused beads kit from my uncle for Christmas. It was quite a rare gift at the time, and the fused beads from that first set traveled with me for years in various bracelet forms.

For the next 10–15 years I forgot about the existence of these little pixel-like beauties only to rediscover them at the age of 26 when I was searching for quirky jewelry to fit my unique style. I couldn't find what I was after in any of the stores I visited. And then it hit me... why don't I make the jewelry myself? Something that's different, bold, and colorful.

If someone had told me 15 years ago that I would still be playing around with beads as I approached age 30, I would've thought they were mad. It turns out that you can never be too old or too young to play with beads. You just need to stay true to yourself. Before I knew it, I was busy creating geeky pixel jewelry for my friends and running my own small-scale jewelry business called Sylph Designs—not to mention, seeing pixels everywhere and in everything.

I've collected lots of awesome projects and pixelated patterns appropriate for kids (and grown-ups!) of all ages in this book. I hope that it will be enough to ignite a spark of passion in you!

Ready to bring some pixel love into your life?

I'd be honored to share my pixel madness and tips and tricks with you going forward as well, so don't hesitate to reach out to me online:

Facebook: www.facebook.com/sylph.designs

Twitter: www.twitter.com/meej2nes and www.twitter.com/SylphDesigns

Pinterest: www.pinterest.com/meej2nes

Instagram: instagram.com/sylphdesigns

Tumblr: sylphdesigns.tumblr.com

Shop: sylphdesigns.etsy.com

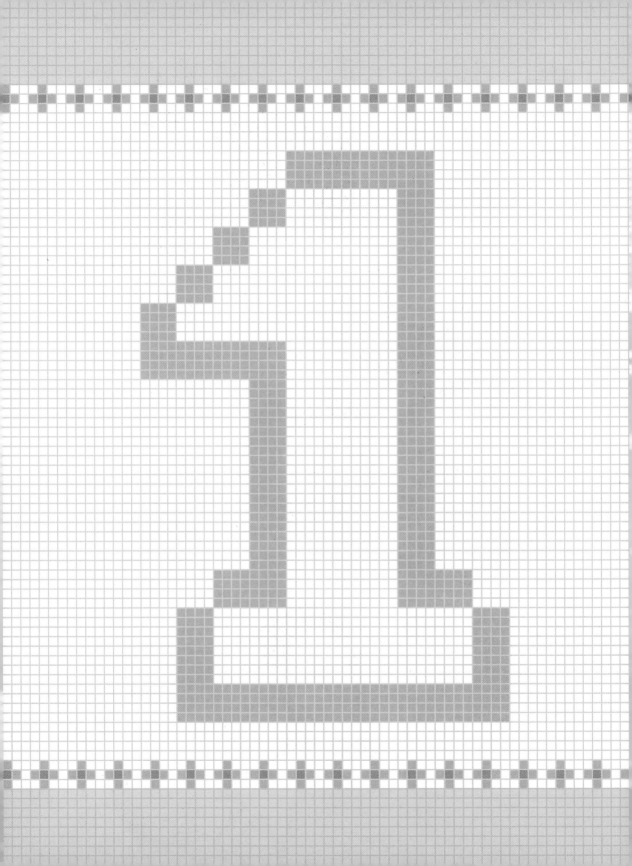

TOOLS, MATERIALS, & TECHNIQUES

TOOLS & MATERIALS

BEFORE YOU START CREATING YOUR FUSE BEAD PROJECTS YOU WILL NEED TO LEARN ABOUT THE TOOLS AND MATERIALS REQUIRED TO COMPLETE THE MOTIFS SHOWN IN THIS BOOK. YOU DON'T NEED A GREAT DEAL OF EQUIPMENT FOR FUSE BEADING, JUST A FEW ESSENTIALS.

BEADS

When starting out with fuse beads, it makes sense to buy a jar or pack of mixed beads, as these are usually inexpensive and are great for practicing your skills before you move on to more elaborate patterns. However, once you start using the patterns, you will most likely want to sort the beads or buy individual colored packs so that it's easier and faster to find the right colors.

SIZES

The standard size of fuse beads is 5 mm (1) in diameter, and they are the most common. They're called midi beads and are suitable from age five and up. Most brands (Hama, Perler, and Nabbi Photo Pearls) carry these as their default sized fuse beads. Although they look the same, the quality can vary between these brands and the lesser-known brands (Pyssla and Melty).

Maxi beads measure 10 mm in diameter and are ideally suited for small children. Mini beads (2) are half the size of the midis at 2.5 mm and allow you to get a more detailed design in a smaller size.

Most of the projects here can be created with either mini or midi beads.

COLORS

Fuse beads come in a wide variety of colors, including solid, translucent, pastel, glitter, and even glow-in-the-dark! Not all colors are made in all sizes, so sometimes you may have to replace the colors depending on which size you're using. You can also try to mix and match between different brands in the same size (Perler, Nabbi Photo Pearls, and Hama work well together).

To find out which colors your favorite brand carries, you should open their website and download a color chart to see what's available.

This also proves to be useful when you're planning on ordering a larger amount of individual bead packs.

PEGBOARD

This is a flat plastic board with tiny pegs in it that will hold the beads in place. Although they come in various sizes and shapes, there are only three types that we use in this book: round (3), square (4), and hexagonal (5).

Note that you will need different pegboards depending on the size of the beads you are using—midi ones require a larger size pegboard whereas mini ones can be created with a pegboard with smaller pegs.

You can buy transparent pegboards so that you can just print out a pattern and lay it under your pegboard then place the beads accordingly.

TWEEZERS, SCISSORS, AND NEEDLES

Long tweezers with a pointed end,

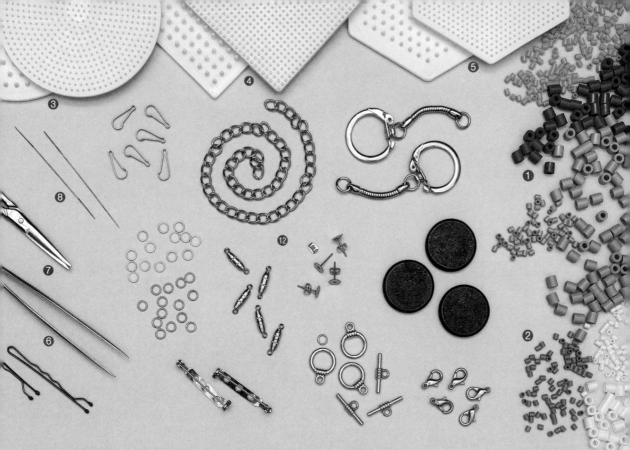

small nail-trimming scissors, and a toothpick—these three items, although not essential, might make your life a little easier when trying to create a pattern on a pegboard. This is particularly true when using mini fuse beads (2.5 mm).

Tweezers (6) and scissors (7) help you pick up the beads from their edges, or they can be used to grab the center hole.

Alternatively, if you want to collect more than one bead at a time, you can dampen a toothpick (which provides purchase for the beads), slide multiple beads onto it, and then work the beads onto the pegboard.

Beading needles (8) are used for beadweaving techniques such as peyote (see pages 18–19).

PLIERS

Pliers are useful tools for attaching findings and can be used to open and close jump rings. To open jump rings

it is best to use a combination of flat-nose (9) and round-nose pliers (10).

To cut different types of chain or wire you'll need wire cutters. These have a sharp edge that allows you to cut through metal easily.

IRON

For the melting part of the process you will need a standard clothes iron with variable heat settings to melt the pattern together. Smaller travel irons are also suitable, as they are easy to hold and control.

PARCHMENT PAPER

You will need parchment paper (11) to cover your pattern to prevent the beads from melting onto the iron. This can be bought from bead retailers, or you can just as easily use wax paper.

FINDINGS

Jewelry findings (12) are the parts

that you'll need in order to turn your finished fused designs into jewelry—be it for earrings, hair clips and pins, necklaces or bracelets, fridge magnets, key chains, or brooches.

ADHESIVES

Depending on what you decide to do with your fuse bead motif, you may want to adhere it to a fabric backing and finding. Some people prefer to use a glue gun for this job or will choose to use Super Glue instead. Guidance is provided on the project pages for the best method.

FABRIC

Felt (13) or ultrasuede can be attached to the back of a motif to disguise a finding or glue residue. Adding a fabric backing to projects such as bobby pins is usually a good idea so as to prevent dried glue from coming into contact with hair.

TECHNIQUES

THE SECRET TO A GREAT FINISHED DESIGN IS TO MASTER THE WHOLE CREATION PROCESS. TO GET YOU STARTED LET'S HAVE A LOOK AT ALL THE DIFFERENT TECHNIQUES THAT YOU'LL NEED TO GET THE PERFECT OUTCOME EVERY TIME.

HOW TO FOLLOW A DESIGN

Once you've settled on a pattern or design you'd like to try, you should prepare your workstation. Find a flat surface to work on and place a cotton towel under your pegboard.

1. Find all the beads in the colors you'd like to use for the design. Don't be afraid to replace the colors used in the original design with ones that you like better. After all, it's your creation!

2. Pour the beads into little bowls (those used for soy sauce with sushi are perfect) or small bead storage containers next to the pegboard.

3. Begin with the outline of the design and then fill it from top to bottom. For circular or hexagonal designs, it is best to work from the center, outward. You may decide to use different colors all at once, but sometimes it makes more sense to add colors one at a time.

4. To make the process quicker when using the mini beads, you can pour a small amount of beads onto the pegboard and move them around using tweezers. This way you won't lose time taking a bead from the bowl and placing it onto the pegboard.

5. When working with midi beads you can do the same thing, only this time hold the beads in your hand and place them with your fingers one color at a time.

FUSING YOUR DESIGN

The heat setting of the iron is very important: for mini beads you should set your iron to a low/medium heat, whereas for midi beads you can use a higher heat setting.

Do not apply too much pressure when melting the patterns created with mini beads or they'll flatten too much. Because they're more fragile to work with than midi beads, you'll need to practice a few times before you get the right time-and-pressure ratio for the design to come out perfectly.

MIXING BRANDS

If you want to mix and match beads of the same size, but from different brands (Perler, Nabbi Photo Pearls, and Hama work well together) it is advisable to do a test before you create the final design. Melting temperatures can differ between brands and this will result in an uneven finish.

GETTING THE LOOK

There are a couple of choices to make when ironing designs together, and these will impact the final look of your fuse bead piece.

The longer the beads are ironed, the flatter they become. Eventually, the hole in the center will disappear completely, leaving a square-looking dot. Melting the design up to this point will give it greater durability and flexibility, but will also alter the look of the design.

Ironing on just one side of the design is suitable for projects where you'll be gluing the melted side onto something flat, or where you don't need to bend the design. Melting on both sides will be great for projects where you need to attach findings to the design, or where you're planning on bending the design.

HOW TO IRON YOUR DESIGN

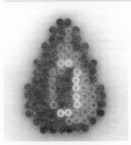

1. Place the parchment paper over your design on the pegboard, ensuring that all the beads are completely covered.

2. Set your iron to the appropriate heat setting and carefully place the iron on top of the design. As the beads start to melt, they will appear darker through the paper, which means they are ready. Be careful not to lift the parchment paper too early when checking. For mini beads, melt for at least 5–7 seconds before you remove the iron. For midi beads, melt for at least 10 seconds before you remove the iron to check the design. Continue if needed.

3. When the first round of ironing is done, flip the pegboard onto a flat surface with the parchment paper side facing down on the table, and remove the pattern from the pegboard. If the beads were melted sufficiently, the design should stick to the parchment paper and hold together, and should come off the pegboard quite easily. If you've melted the design for too long, it might stick to the pegboard, in which case, use a toothpick or tweezers to carefully remove the design from the pegboard.

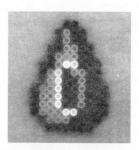

4. This is your chance to melt the beads again. Cover the other side of the design with a second piece of parchment paper, place the design on a heatproof surface, and repeat the melting process. As the beads are already warm from the first round of melting, you should only iron the pattern for half as long as you did initially.

5. After ironing, the beads will remain hot for a short while, so handle them with tweezers. If your final design should be flat, you can place a heavy object, such as a book, on the design to keep it from bending while it's cooling. If your final design should be bent, then this is the time to do it using a heat-resistant object such as a glass. Hold the design in the desired position and allow it to cool completely.

6. Once it has cooled you can remove the design, and it should hold its shape. If you are not satisfied with the outcome, or weren't able to position it quickly enough, you can heat it up again by repeating the ironing process. Be careful not to flatten the design too much or to melt the beads for too long.

CLEANING THE IRON

- If you accidentally melt some of the beads onto the iron, the first thing you should do is try getting them off by rubbing the iron onto a cloth that you don't mind getting dirty.
- Failing that, unplug the iron and allow it to cool off. Use a wooden toothpick to remove the melted plastic. You can also use a damp sponge to aid removal.
- Don't use sharp objects such as a knife or a fork that could damage the iron. Best practice is to always be attentive and keep the parchment paper in between the design and the iron.

WHAT NOT TO DO

- Don't use a high temperature setting to melt mini beads—this will result in a really quick melting process and will end up flattening and ruining your design.
- Don't apply too much pressure to the iron while melting; this will result in an uneven finish, as one side of the design will be more melted than the other.
- Do not melt away all the center holes when you're working with a project where you'll need to use the holes to attach findings (using jump rings).

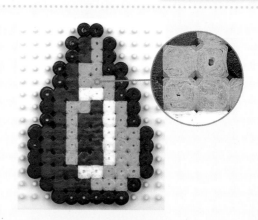

ATTACHING FINDINGS

There is a whole host of findings out there to help you transform your fuse bead motifs into wearable pieces. Here you will learn a number of the basic techniques to take your motifs to the next level.

OPENING AND CLOSING JUMP RINGS

1. Grip each side of the ring with a pair of pliers and twist the ends away from each other, creating an empty space in the ring.

2. Thread the open ring through the hole in the fuse bead. Twist the ends of the jump ring back toward each other so that the ends meet.

3. Once you've added the desired finding, you can hide the connecting part of the jump ring in the bead. This will prevent it from coming loose when wearing the design.

GLUING DESIGNS TO FINDINGS

If you'd like to turn your motif into a brooch, you can either glue the brooch back straight onto the design or use felt or ultrasuede to hide the brooch back. Both of these techniques work better if one side of your design has been melted flat so that the holes are no longer visible. This will also prevent the glue from seeping through onto the visible side of the design.

ATTACH A BROOCH BACK TO A DESIGN USING GLUE

Make sure one side of the design is melted as flat as possible without ruining the design. Add Super Glue to both the flat side of the design as well as the brooch back and push them together. Apply pressure (consult the glue manufacturer's instructions for how long) and then leave it to dry.

Alternatively, you can use a hot glue gun to do the same thing; however, in this scenario you should not flatten the side of the design that you are going to glue; this is because the hot glue used in a glue gun will join more effectively with the design if it has some bead centers to adhere to.

TO ATTACH AND HIDE BROOCH BACKS WITH FABRIC

1. Cut a piece of felt or ultrasuede to the size of your design.

2. Place the brooch back onto the piece of fabric and mark the places where the two ends of the brooch back touch the fabric. Take the scissors and cut into the fabric on those two ends. The holes don't need to be too big, just large enough for each end of the brooch back to push through.

3. Take the brooch back and push the ends through the fabric. Start from the end where the pin is attached.

4. Once both sides have been pushed through fabric, add glue to the side of the design that was melted flat and place the fabric with the brooch back onto the design. Apply pressure and leave it to dry. The fabric will help both to hide the brooch back and to join the brooch back to the design.

ADDING MAGNETS

Before attaching magnets, make sure your design has completely cooled off and has been fused together properly on both sides. You can melt one side slightly more to help the Super Glue stick better.

1. Choose where you're going to glue the magnet(s). If you place a magnet too far away from the top of the design, it may be too top heavy and won't stay upright when sticking to a metal surface.

2. Use the nozzle of the Super Glue tube or a toothpick to cover the magnet with a thin layer of glue and let the glue dry for one minute.

3. Apply a second coat of glue; using two coats helps the adhesion. Hold the design face-up and press magnet onto desired area on the back for a few seconds. If you lay the design face down to glue the magnet onto it, the glue can seep through the holes and leave an ugly residue on the front of your design.

4. Let the glue dry completely before adding any additional magnets, or the magnets will not stay in place.

5. Once you've added all the magnets, let the finished pieces dry overnight. Never bend your designs, or the magnets may fall off.

ATTACH A FABRIC-BACKED DESIGN ONTO A BOBBY PIN

1. Cut a piece of felt or ultrasuede to the size of your design.

2. Take the fabric and push it in between the bobby pin and center it, pull it to the end of the bobby pin.

3. Place a dab of glue onto one side of the fabric (on the side of the ridged end of the bobby pin) and onto the design. Push the two together. Apply some pressure and leave it to dry. The fabric will help hide the glued side of the fabric and connects the bobby pin to the design.

ATTACH A DESIGN ONTO A BOBBY PIN WITH JUST GLUE

Using a hot glue gun, place a dab of glue on the motif. Press the motif onto the bobby pin and make sure that you have the design positioned correctly, so that the pattern is oriented the way you want it.

Different bead sizes
This matroyoshka doll pattern (see page 86) has been made up in both 2.5 mm beads (left) and 5 mm beads (right) and is shown at actual size.

BEADWEAVING WITH PEYOTE STITCH

Peyote stitch, also known as brick stitch, is one of the easiest beadweaving techniques to start with and it's ideal to use with fuse beads. Although it can seem tricky at first, the stitch is based on a simple pattern of making spaces in your work and then filling those spaces with beads.

EVEN-COUNT PEYOTE STITCH

ADDING A STOP BEAD

You can add a stop bead to the thread at the start of your work to help with tension and also to stop the beads you'll add from falling off the thread. Simply pick up a bead, position it where needed, and circle through it a few times. Make sure you thread through it enough times so that it doesn't slide off, but not so many that it will be hard to remove later on.

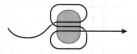

1. Cut a length of thread (nylon fishing line, 0.5 mm) suitable for working with (not too long). Add a stopping bead about 4 in (10 cm) from the beginning of the thread. Pick up an even number of beads (the number of beads you pick up will determine the width of your work). These beads will form the first two rows of peyote stitch.

2. To bead row 3, pick up one bead (if using two colors then pick up one in the second color). Skipping the last bead added in Step 1, take the needle and thread back through the next bead along.

3. Pick up one more bead (again in the second color), and skipping the next bead added in Step 1, thread through the next one along. You are now threading through the beads that will make up row 2 and ignoring those that will form row 1.

4. Continue adding beads in exactly the same way all along the row. The total number of beads you add will be half the amount you picked up in Step 1.

5. You are now changing direction again to begin beading the fourth row. Pick up one new bead (in the first color) and thread through the last bead you added in the previous row.

6. Repeat adding single beads (of the first color) all along the row until you have filled all the spaces. Then change direction and continue in this manner until your work is as long as desired. As you work, make sure the beads are always pushed up firmly and the design is flat to keep it nice and even.

UNEVEN-COUNT PEYOTE STITCH

This is beaded in almost the same way as even-count, but it has a figure-eight turn at the end of every other row.

1. Add a stop bead. Pick up an odd number of beads (just as with even-count peyote, the number of beads you pick up will determine the width of your work; these beads will form the first two rows).

2. Using regular peyote stitch, bead all the way along the row until you can't easily add another bead.

3. You now need to turn so you can fill in the missing bead and be in a position to continue. Without picking up a new bead, thread down through the next bead along that sits in the first row (the first bead you picked up).

4. Pick up one new bead (the last bead in row 3). Thread through the second bead in from the edge of your work (the last bead in row 2) and the lowest bead of the next pair (second to last bead of row 1). The third row is now finished.

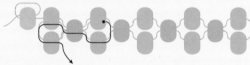

5. Thread through the bead above the one you are currently exiting (pointing back toward the end of the row). Thread through the next two beads along to reach the edge and then thread back through the last new bead added (pointing toward the body of the piece).

6. Continue beading using regular peyote stitch, remembering that you only have to perform this turn at the end of every other row.

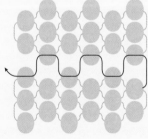

ZIPPING UP

Once you finish your peyote band, you will need to join the ends to make a loop. This is done by interlocking or "zipping up" the beads of the two ends and weaving the thread through these beads to secure them together.

Instead of adding new beads to the spaces in your design, you will use the other end of your band to fill in the gaps. Once you've threaded the two sides together, remove the stop bead and tie a knot between the two ends to tighten them. Now you can hide the ends in your project and cut the ends off.

ADDING AND FINISHING THREADS

The basic method for adding and finishing threads is to weave them securely into your work, making sure they cross over themselves and are held tight. In this diagram, the black thread is the old one, and the red thread is the new one being woven in, ready to continue.

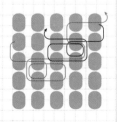

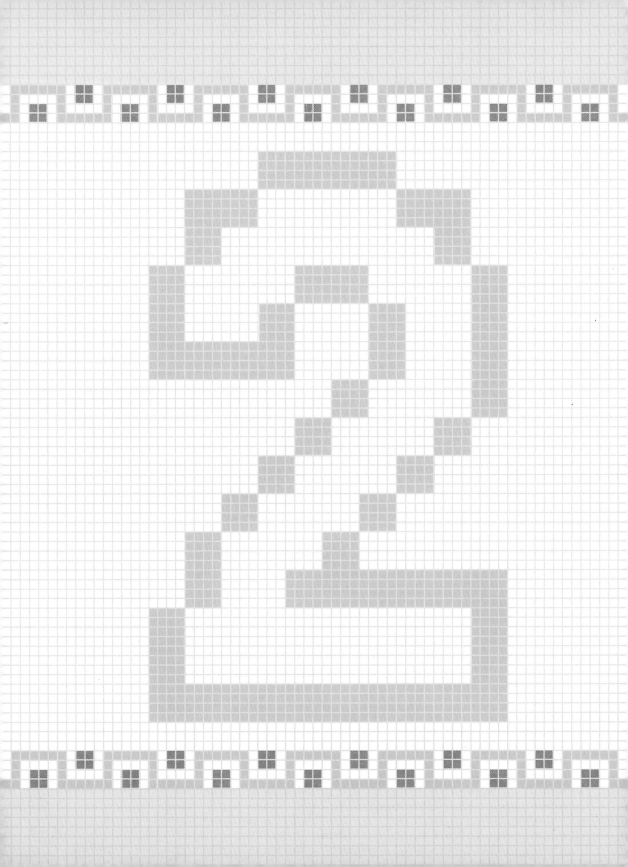

THE PATTERNS

SPRING

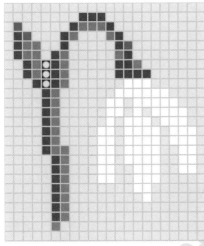

(79) 30 34 40 (3)

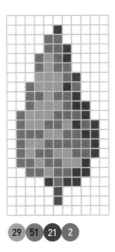

29 51 21 2

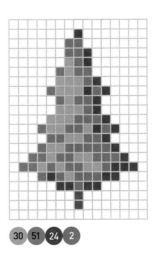

30 51 24 2

seasons

68
22
(7)

133
14
22

154
15
30

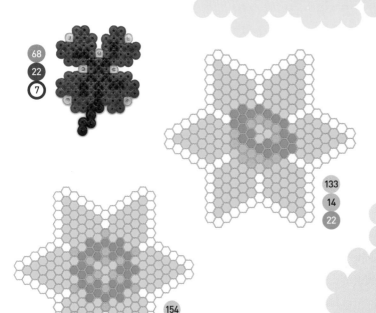

INFO! Each motif in this chapter has been made up using 2.5 mm beads and is shown at approximately actual size. If you decide to create the motif using 5 mm beads, your finished design will be twice the size of the chart or sample featured here.

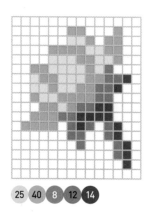

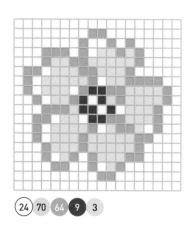

25 40 8 12 14

24 70 64 9 3

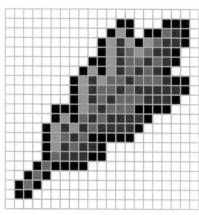

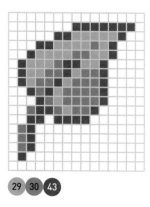

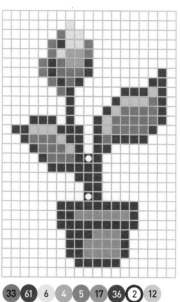

19 35 47 62

29 30 43

33 61 6 4 5 17 36 2 12

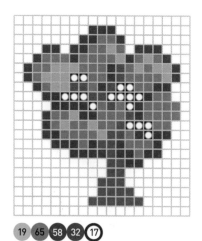

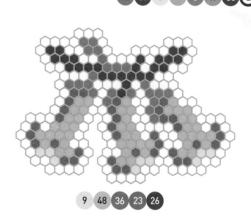

19 65 58 32 17

9 48 36 23 26

summer

(11) (61) (17) (42) (23) (23)

(28) (22) (161) (208)

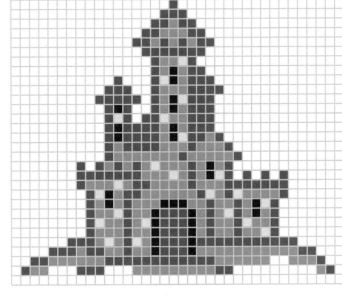

(35) (94) (41)

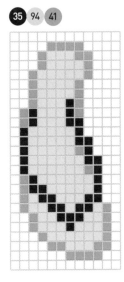

(5) (98) (20) (4) (81)

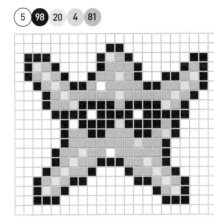

(4) (76) (20) (6) (100)

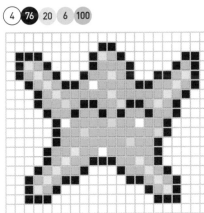

(48) (48) (28) (25) (2) (2) (6) (6)

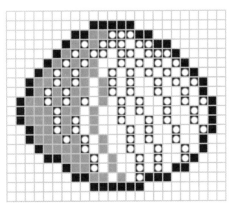

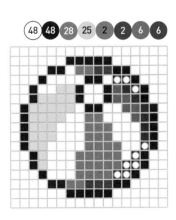

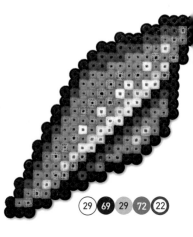

(29) (69) (29) (72) (22)

(89) (51) (53) (86)

FALL

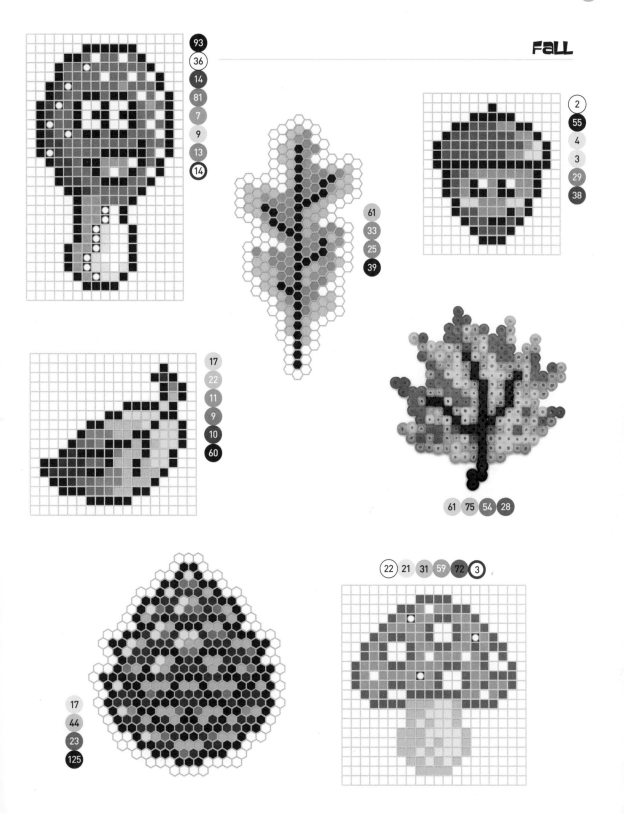

WINTER

78 29

71 42

60 14 16 3 4
6 9 21

88 30

90 30

43 44 28 20

113 99

55
54
31

24
33
52
13
19
27

19
87
96
11
90
11

FLOWERS

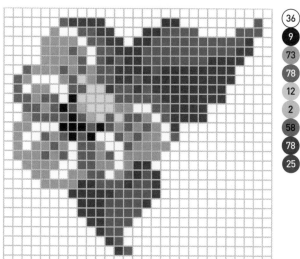

36
9
73
78
12
2
58
78
25

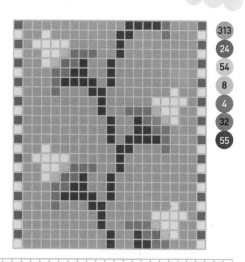

313
24
54
8
4
32
55

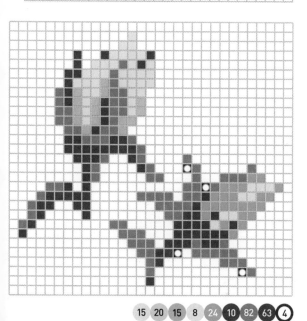

15 20 15 8 24 10 82 63 4

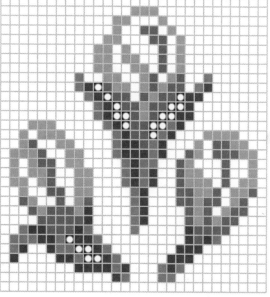

63 102 86 47 62 19

30 7 24 42

8 5 80 16 32 12 16

5 38 40 60 5 35 51 21

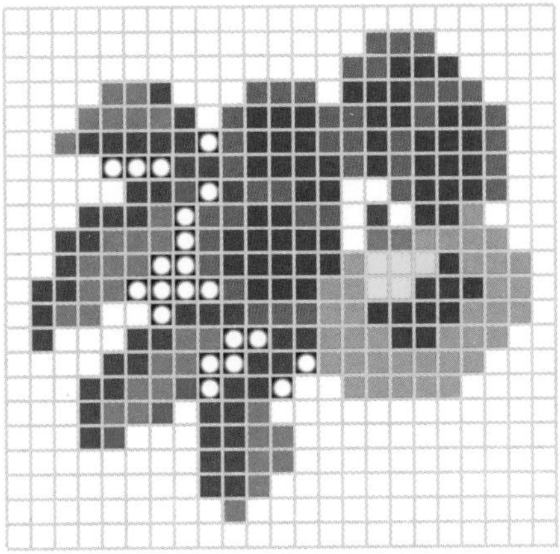

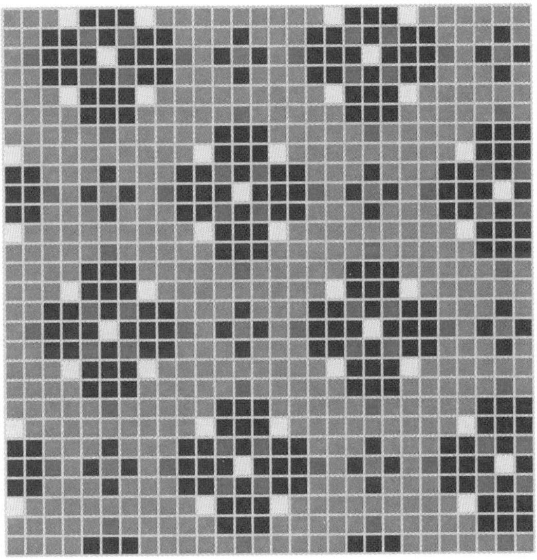

420 40 64 227 8 32

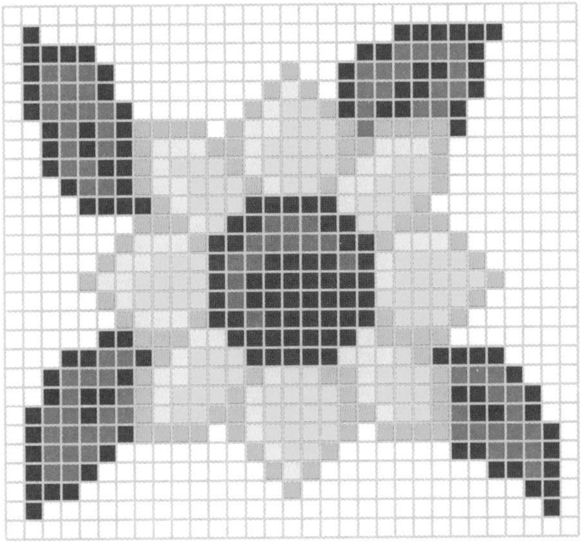

57 99 90 70 65 14 56

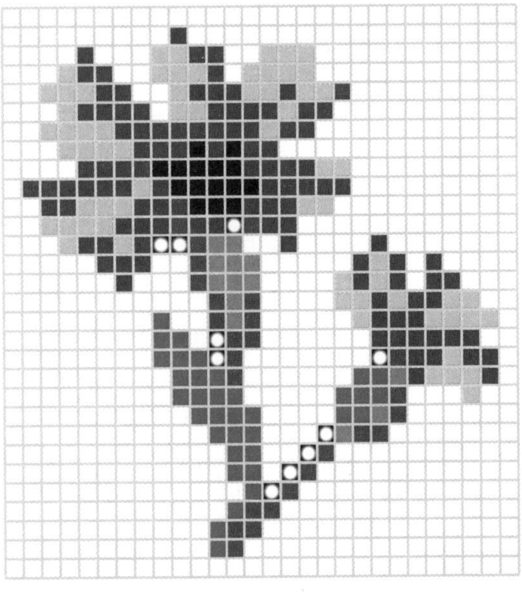

15 66 109 13 35 26 10

14 37 75 107 66 3 55 56

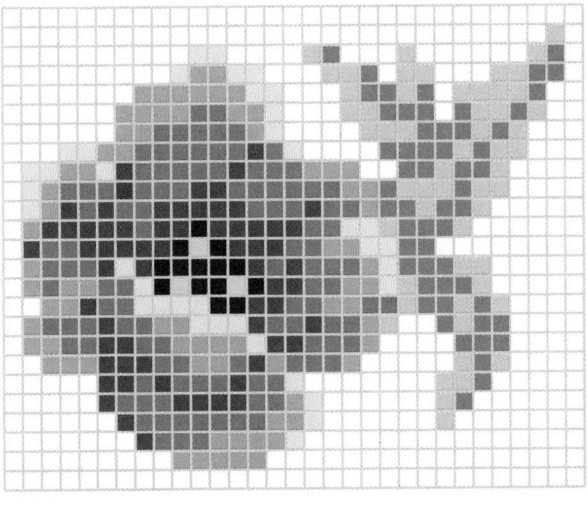

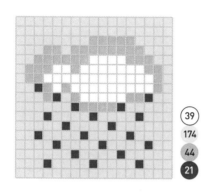

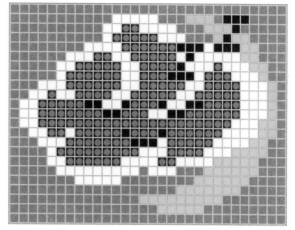

39
174
44
21

138 31 68 169

92 75 15 31 17 16 15 16 15 16

WEATHER

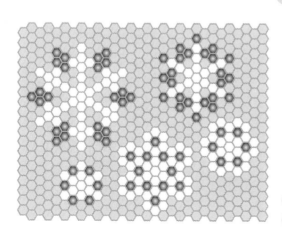

131
72

51
48

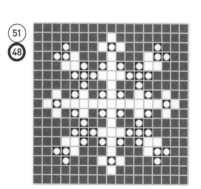

209 51 16 13

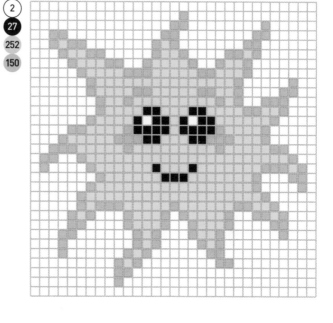

2
27
252
150

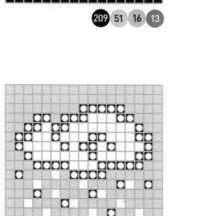

57 173 59

10
23
43
34

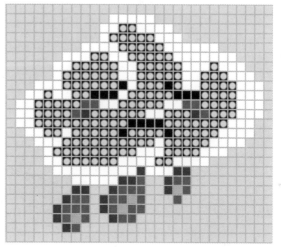

142 14 4 28 19 167

TIP! When you're creating small items, such as these raindrops, it's best to place more than one at a time on the pegboard. This will balance the iron a little bit and will prevent the design from becoming too flat.

MUSIC

(42) (3)

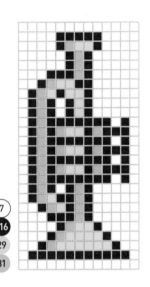

(7)
(116)
(29)
(31)

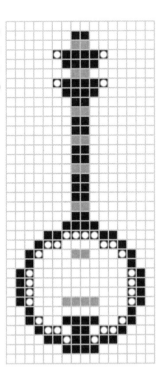

(72)
(80)
(18)
(30)

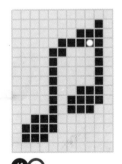

(41) (1)

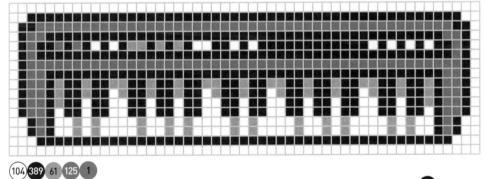

(104) (389) (61) (125) (1)

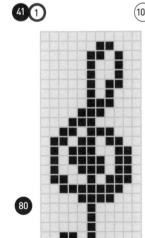

(80)

(20) (135) (20)

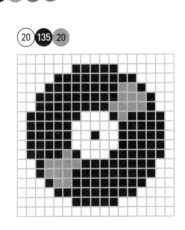

(86)
(50)
(6)
(4)
(4)
(6)
(10)

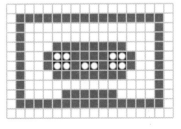

(70)
(74)
(10)

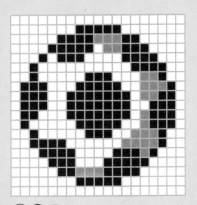

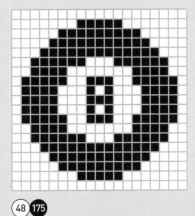

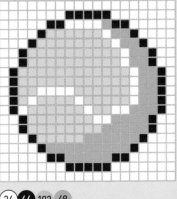

24 44 103 49

67 130 25

48 175

92 31 32

SPORT

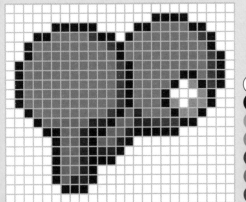

5
80
7
136
16
23
16

28 10 34 6 3 49

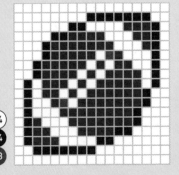

44
44
93

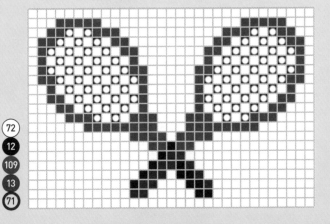

72
12
109
13
71

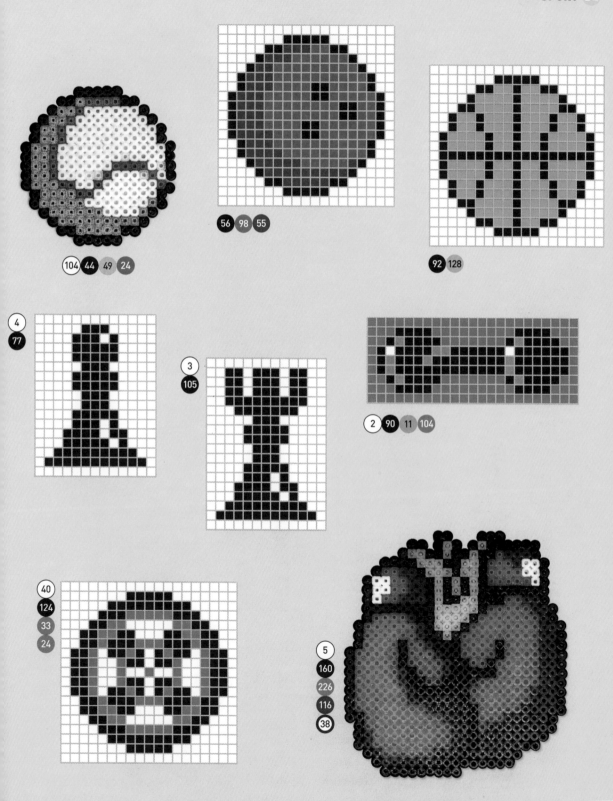

24
41
65
34
37
94

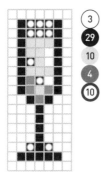

1
29
6
14
15

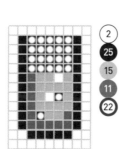

2
25
15
11
22

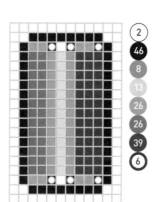

2
46
8
13
26
26
39
6

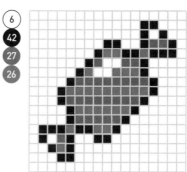

5
29
16
5
42

3
29
10
4
10

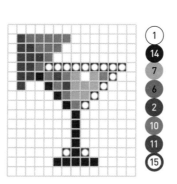

1
14
7
6
2
10
11
15

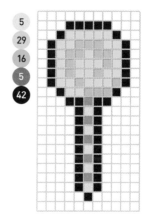

6
42
27
26

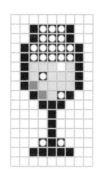

1
28
13
2
20

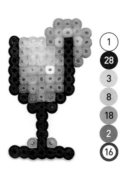

1
28
3
8
18
2
16

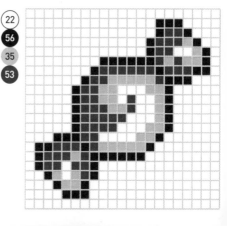

22
56
35
53

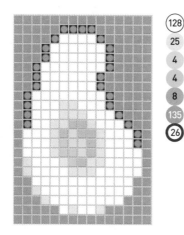

128
25
4
4
8
135
26

11 20 13 27 9 9 68 16 59

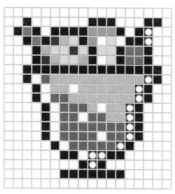

16 71 6 4 4 4
30 28 2 3 13 4

25 5
10 6
6 15
8 38
8

14 38 18 5 4
6 5 12 14

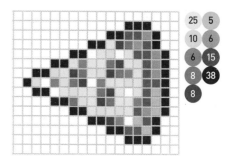

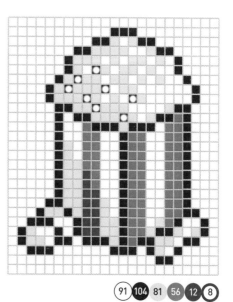

20
49
20
32
10
17
24

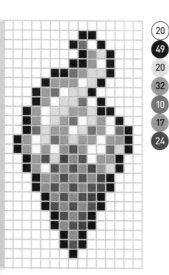

I almost melted!

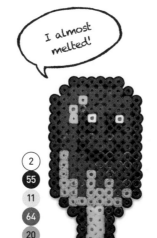

2
55
11
64
20

91 104 81 56 12 8

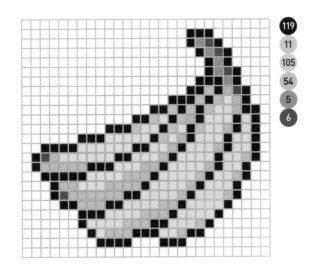

119
11
105
54
5
6

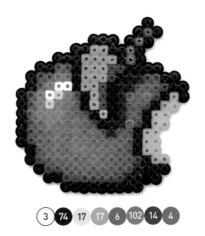

3 74 17 17 6 102 14 4

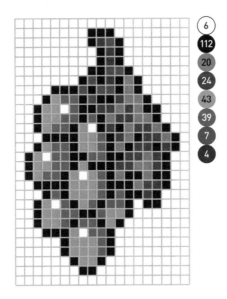

6
112
20
24
43
39
7
4

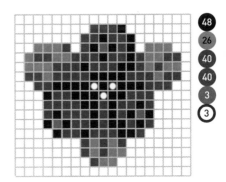

48
26
40
40
3
3

40 13 53 23 30

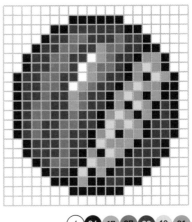

4 84 17 37 98 13 21

Seriously squeezable!

9
107
13
10
61
66
7
9

18 92 20 177 67 5

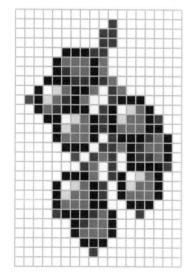

6 53 13 52

5 82 10 23 10 42 11 7

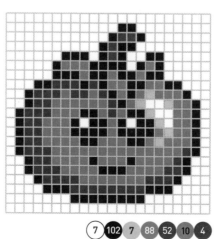
7 102 7 88 52 10 4

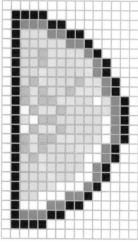

22 55 43 61 22 29

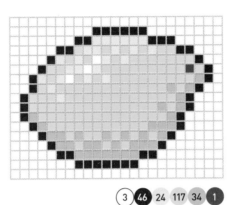

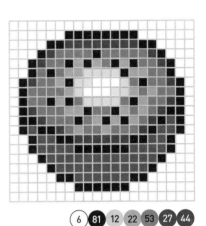

64　10　25　7　34
60　19　25　22

3　46　24　117　34　1

6　81　12　22　53　27　44

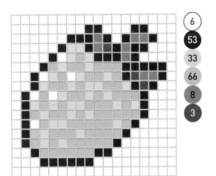

6
53
33
66
8
3

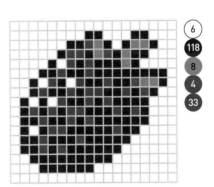

6
118
8
4
33

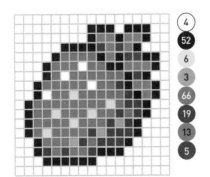

4
52
6
3
66
19
13
5

TIP! Simply by changing the colorway of this design you can create three different types of berry: cloudberry, raspberry, and blackberry.

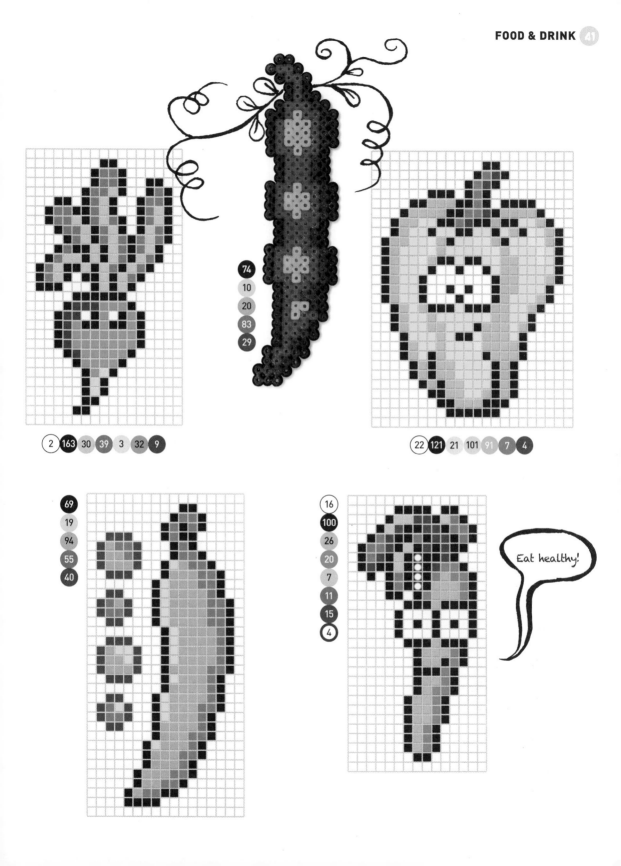

Eat healthy!

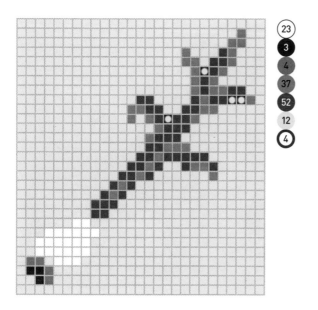

23
3
4
37
52
12
4

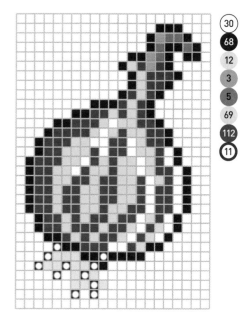

30
68
12
3
5
69
112
11

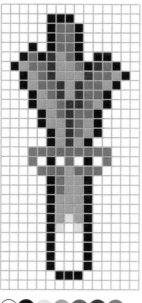

17 59 3 38 31 15 18

58 10 52 21 8

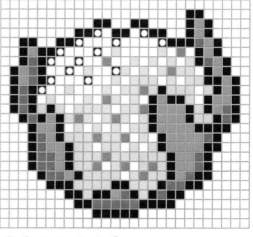

75 124 95 48 32 15 14

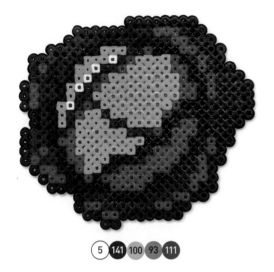

5 141 100 93 111

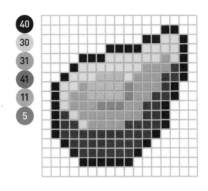

40 30 31 41 11 5

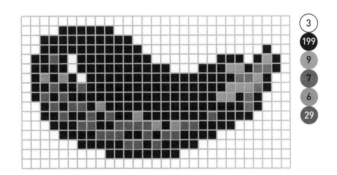

3 199 9 7 6 29

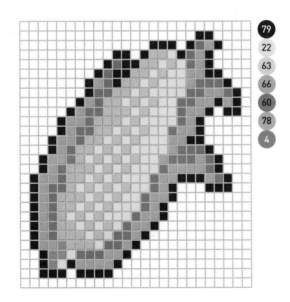

79 22 63 66 60 78 4

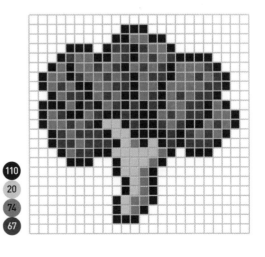

110 20 74 67

18 28 11 44

1 63 18 65

1
13
110
35
11
48
11

1
54
19
5

UNDER THE SEA

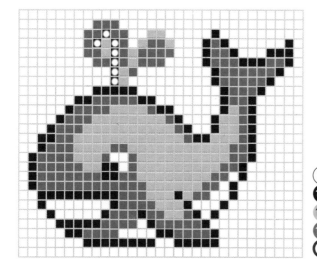

28
104
114
154
7

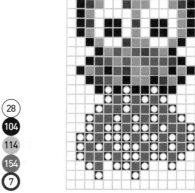

24
47
37
47
18
54

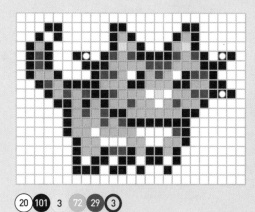

20 101 3 72 29 3

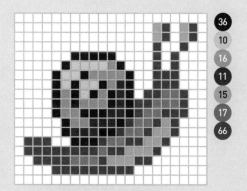

36
10
16
11
15
17
66

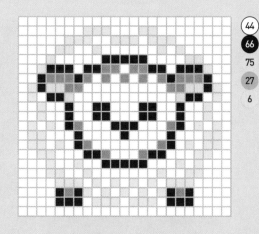

44
66
75
27
6

90
36
6
209

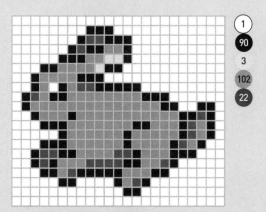

1
90
3
102
22

6
155
49
82
35
35
2

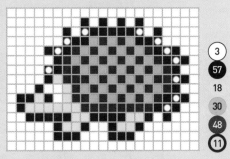

3
57
18
30
48
11

10
98
6
67
38

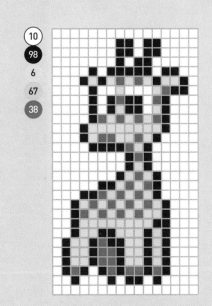

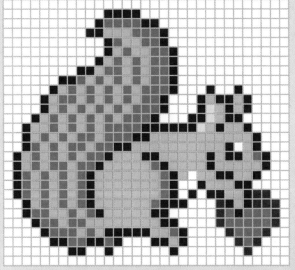

5
127
3
183
136
15

25 143 10 89

Bead it! Iron it! Ribbit!

34
91
4
17
93

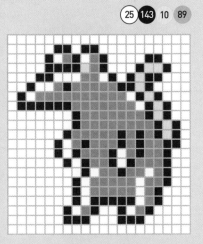

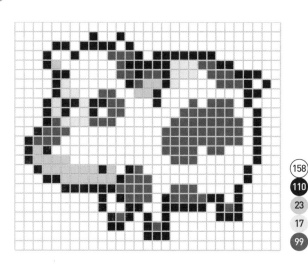

158
110
23
17
99

Bully for you!

72
117
8
61
39

2
35
4
37
57
6
164

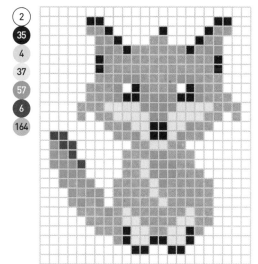

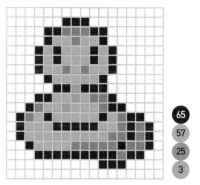

65
57
25
3

No monkey business!

2
108
110
125

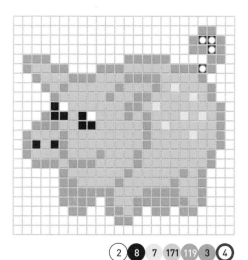

2 8 7 171 119 3 4

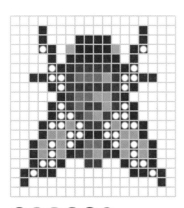

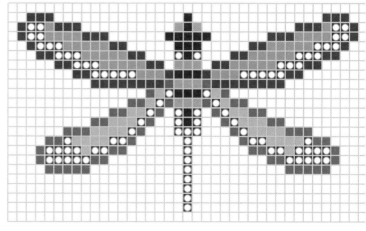

63 14 8 10 26 38

19 11 46 58 32 66 72

INSECTS

34 271 94 146 18

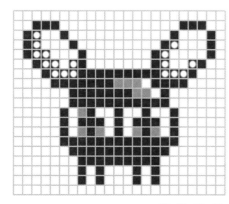

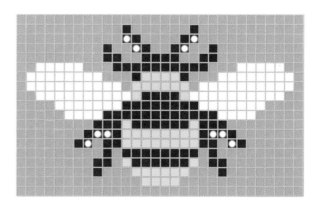

38 123 10 17

88 96 42 10

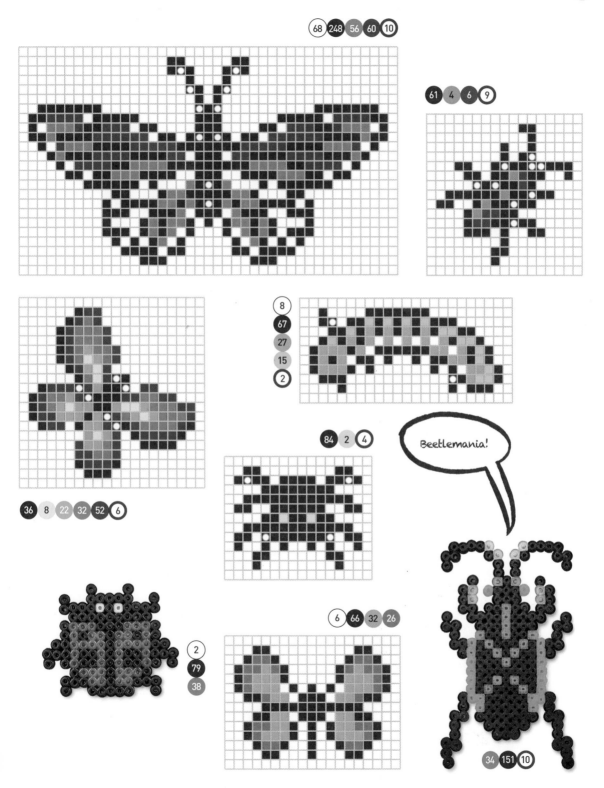

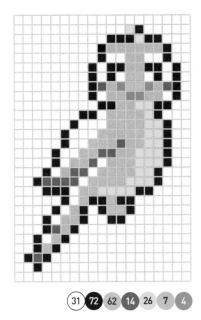

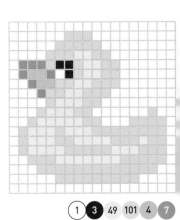

(31) (72) (62) (14) (26) (7) (4)

(1) (3) (49) (101) (4) (7)

(42) (167) (25) (69) (42) (69)

BIRDS

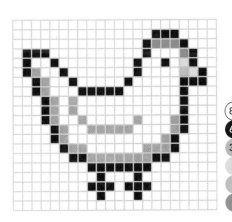

(86)
(65)
(32)
(2)
(1)
(4)

I'm just the coolest bird!

(110)
(163)
(2)
(8)
(18)

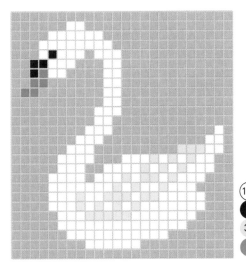

(157)
(4)
(31)
(5)

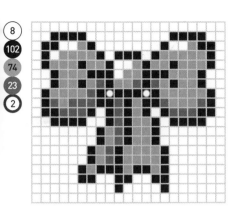

8
102
74
23
2

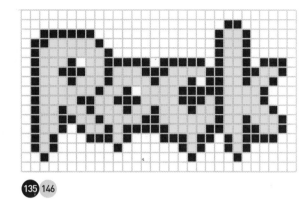

135 146

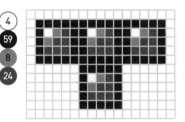

4
59
8
24

GEEK CHIC

3 128 115

6
85
104
34

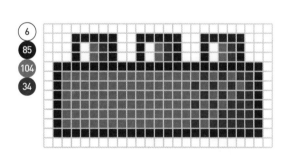

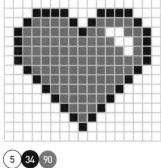

5 34 90

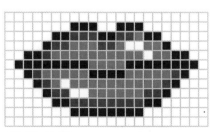

6 56 50 26

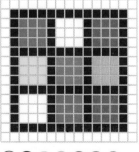

18 88 9 9 18 18 9

SKULLS

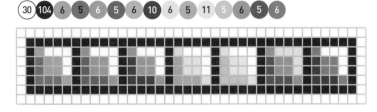

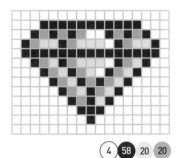

4 · 58 · 20 · 20

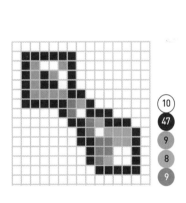

11 · 47 · 24 · 22

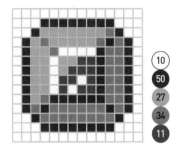

10 · 50 · 27 · 34 · 11

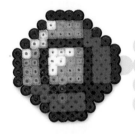

29 · 85 · 23 · 39

BLING

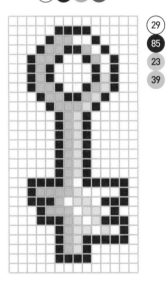

10 · 47 · 9 · 8 · 9

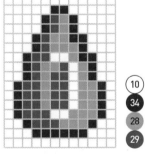

10 · 34 · 28 · 29

43 · 97 · 59 · 39

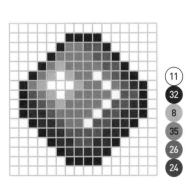

11 · 32 · 8 · 35 · 26 · 24

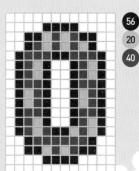

56
20
40

20
44
33

55
23
29

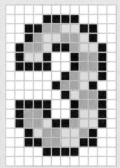

54
24
29

numbers & Letters

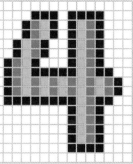

61
29
27

STAND FOR MOTIFS

These numbers would work really well as cake toppers. To stick your created number into a cake you will also need to create a "leg"-part for the number. The "leg" layout has 3 levels:

- Black is suitable for all numbers that end with a bottom of 4 beads.

- Pink will work for number 9, which has a base 5 beads wide.

- Purple is for numbers 1 and 2 which have bases 7 beads wide.

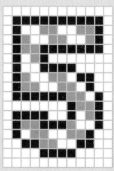

26
64
32

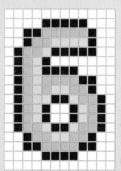

54
22
39

48
10
30

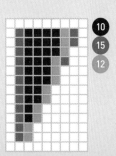

10
15
12

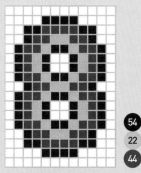

54
22
44

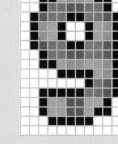

54
17
19
10
15

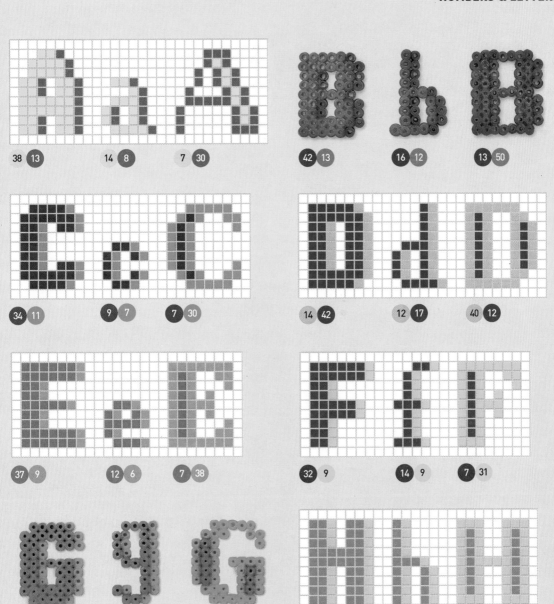

38 13   14 8   7 30

42 13   16 12   13 50

34 11   9 7   7 30

14 42   12 17   40 12

37 9   12 6   7 38

32 9   14 9   7 31

37 13   18 13   8 39

40 16   15 13   14 42

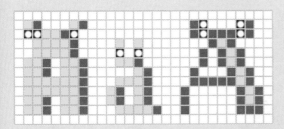

ADDING PUNCTUATION MARKS

If you want to add an apostrophe, accent, umlaut, or
other punctuation mark to a letter you can easily do so.
Leave one row between the letter and your mark and
add in your desired diacritic. If you're creating a letter
with no background, make sure you use translucent
beads to fuse your mark to the letter. Here's an example
using the letter A and an umlaut.

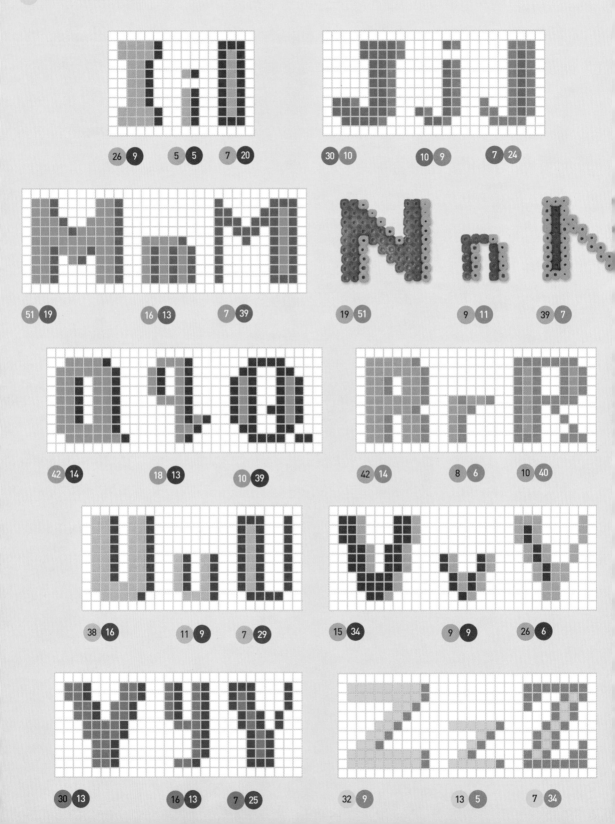

26 9   5 5   7 20

30 10   10 9   7 24

51 19   16 13   7 39   19 51   9 11   39 7

42 14   18 13   10 39   42 14   8 6   10 40

38 16   11 9   7 29   15 34   9 9   26 6

30 13   16 13   7 25   32 9   13 5   7 34

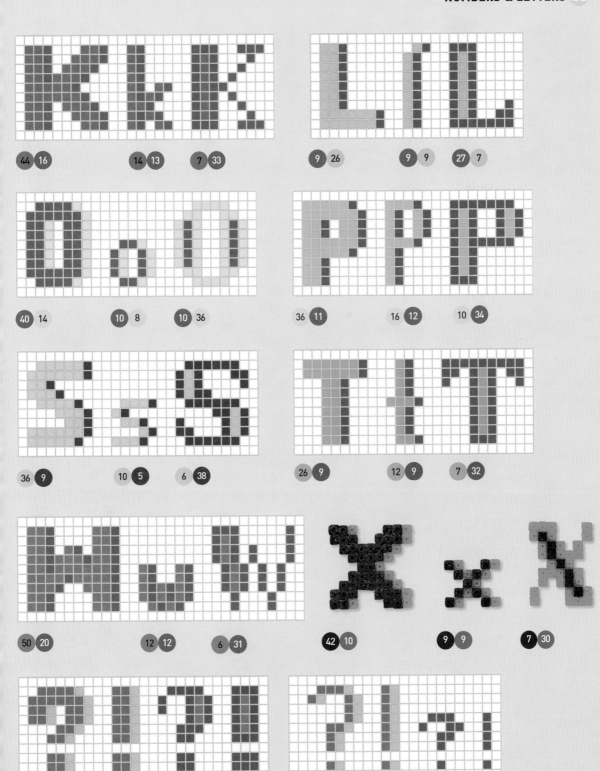

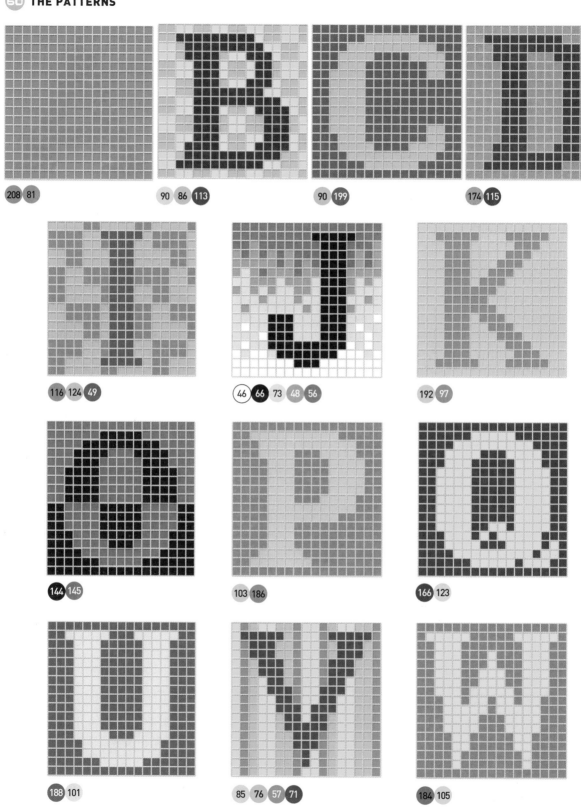

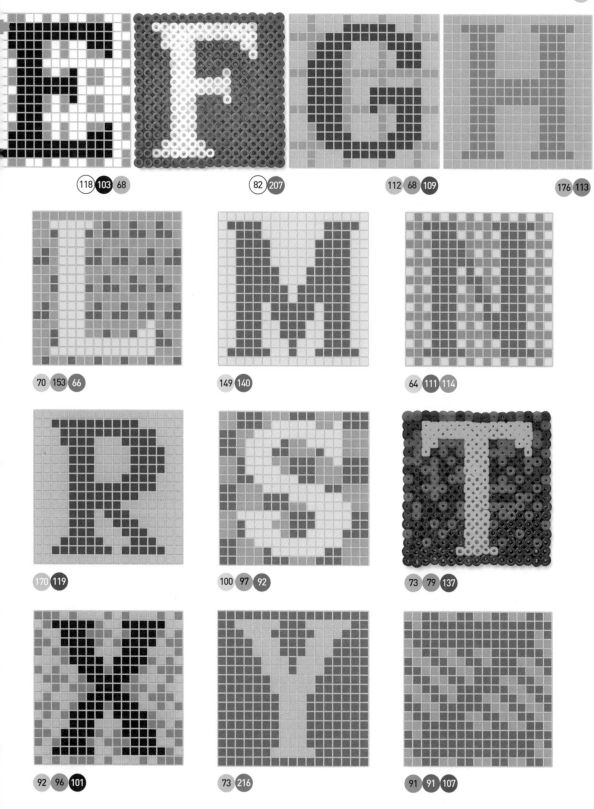

118 103 68

82 207

112 68 109

176 113

70 153 66

149 140

64 111 114

170 119

100 97 92

73 79 137

92 96 101

73 216

91 91 107

emoticons

I'm WAY cool!

| 40 |
| 38 |
| 6 |
| 93 |

| 40 |
| 28 |
| 5 |
| 104 |

GRRR...

| 46 |
| 27 |
| 22 |
| 88 |

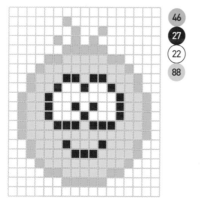

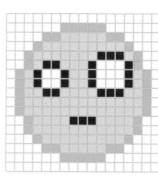

| 40 |
| 23 |
| 13 |
| 101 |

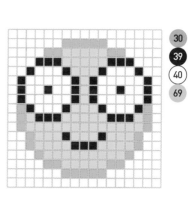

| 30 |
| 39 |
| 40 |
| 69 |

| 40 |
| 34 |
| 28 |
| 75 |

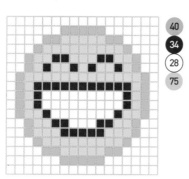

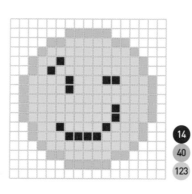

| 14 |
| 40 |
| 123 |

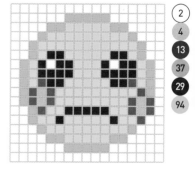

| 2 |
| 4 |
| 13 |
| 37 |
| 29 |
| 94 |

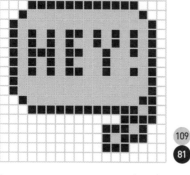

CHAT BUBBLES

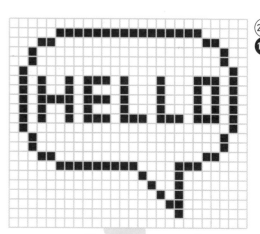

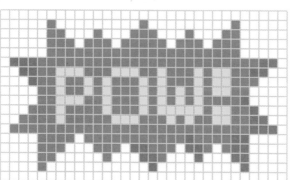

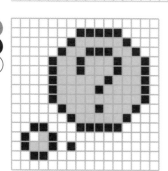

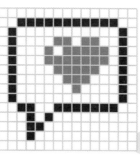

TIP! For the "?" bubble, a background needs to be filled so that the chat bubble will stay intact. Alternatively, you can use translucent beads to fill the void between the dot, small bubble, and big bubble.

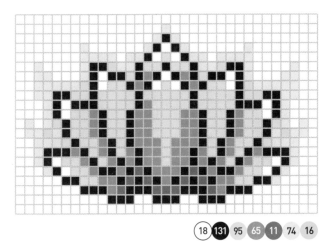

18 131 95 65 11 74 16

8 121 23 42 92 8 5 14

TATTOOS

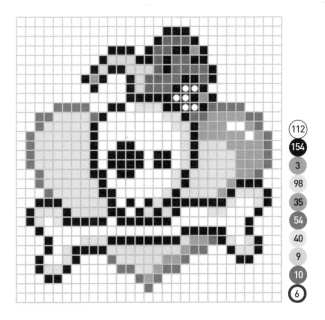

112
154
3
98
35
54
40
9
10
6

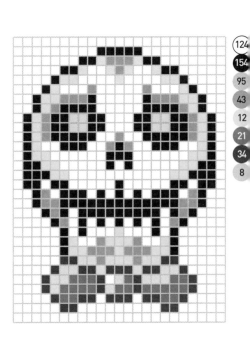

124
154
95
43
12
21
34
8

13 1 26 37 89 71 31 26 37 49

6 76 53 60 77 39 26

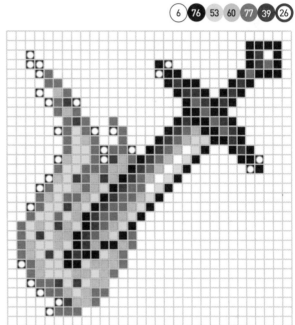

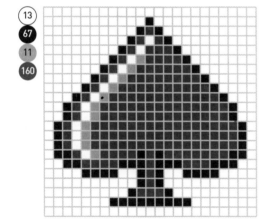

13
67
11
160

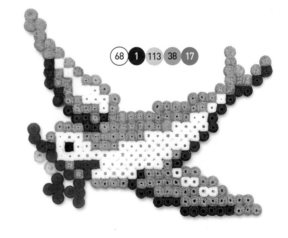

68 1 113 38 17

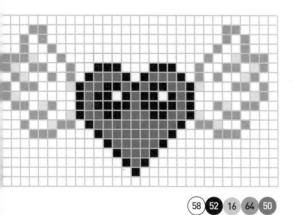

58 52 16 64 50

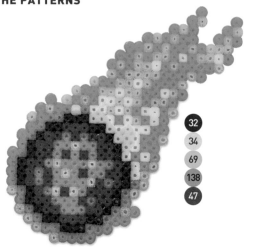

32
34
69
138
47

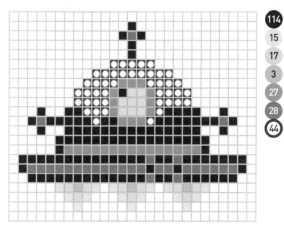

114
15
17
3
27
28
44

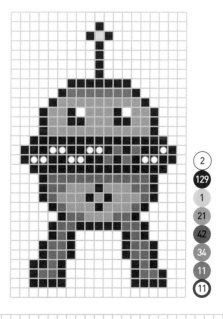

2
129
1
21
42
34
11
11

23
165
39
18
19
86
28

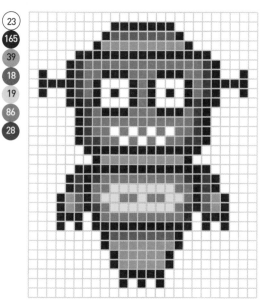

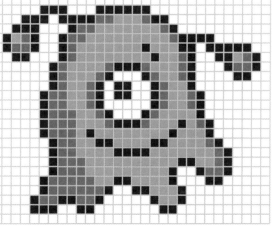

3 17 135 142 82

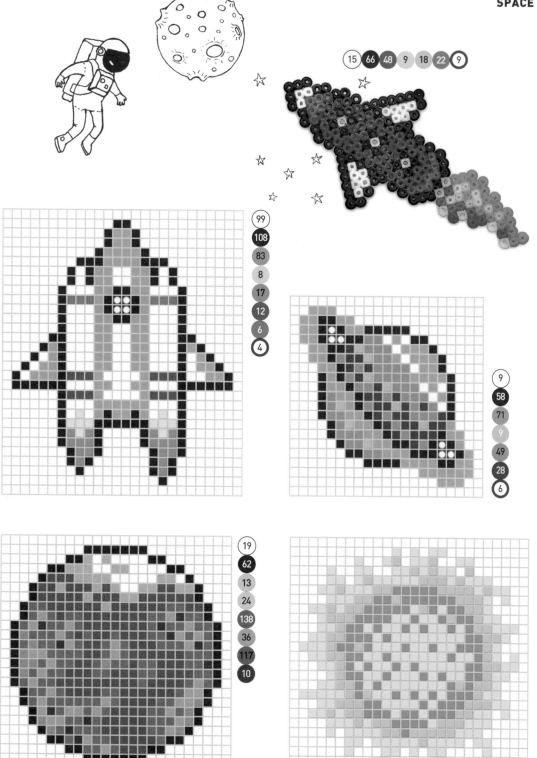

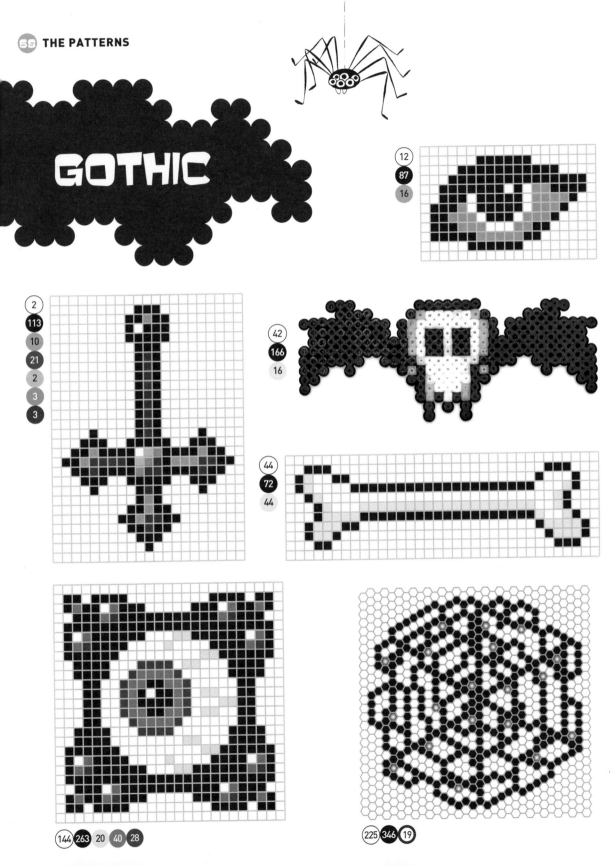

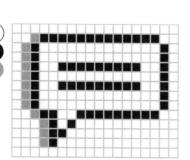

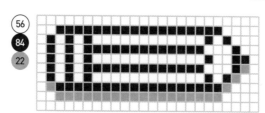

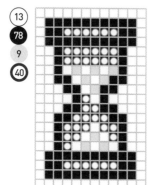

SYMBOLS

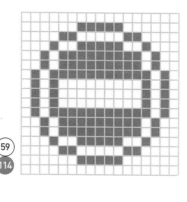

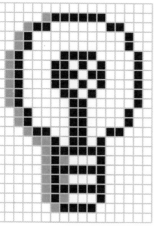

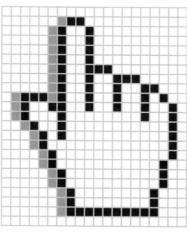

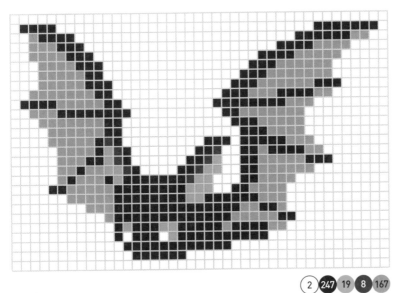

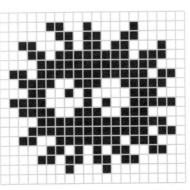

Let's be friends!

8
103
71
59

2 247 19 8 167

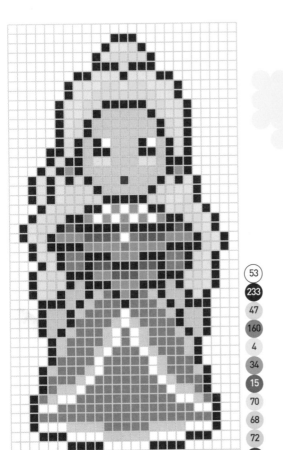

53
233
47
160
4
34
15
70
68
72
1

MYTHICAL CREATURES

22 159

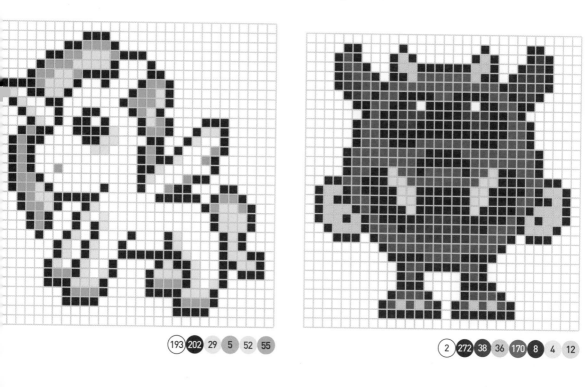

193 202 29 5 52 55

2 272 38 36 170 8 4 12

44 168 21 110 38 14 16 12

I'm feeling a little flat!

14
193
99
85

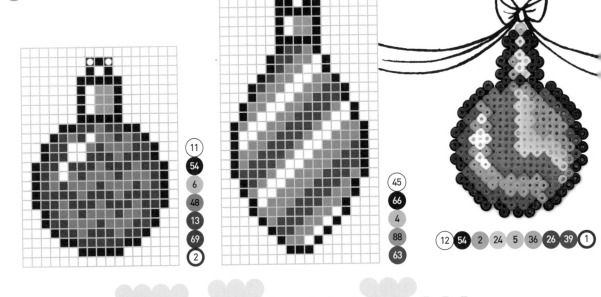

11
54
6
48
13
69
2

45
66
4
88
63

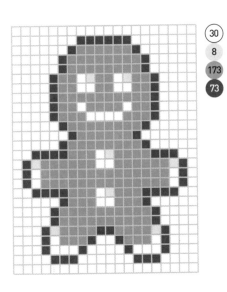

12 54 2 24 5 36 26 39 1

CHRISTMAS

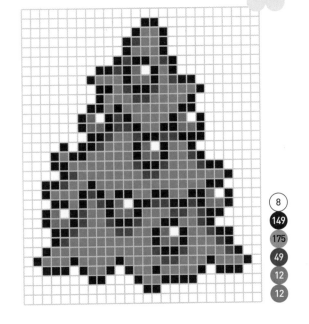

8
149
175
49
12
12

30
8
173
73

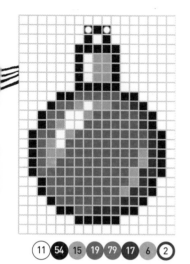

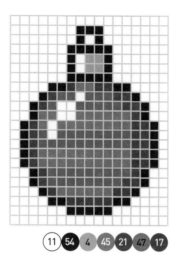

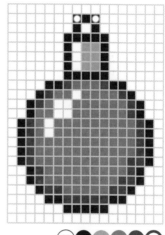

(11) (54) (15) (19) (79) (17) (6) (2)

(11) (54) (4) (45) (21) (47) (17)

(11) (54) (6) (98) (33) (2)

(4) (112) (10) (28) (34) (48)

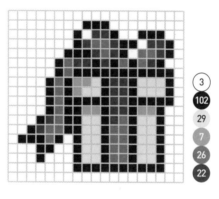

(3) (102) (29) (7) (26) (22)

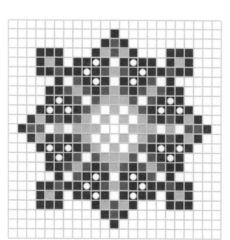

(29) (48) (52) (120) (24)

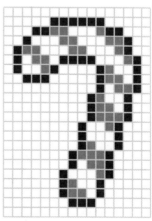

(47) (56) (38)

(10) (48) (6) (30) (44) (10)

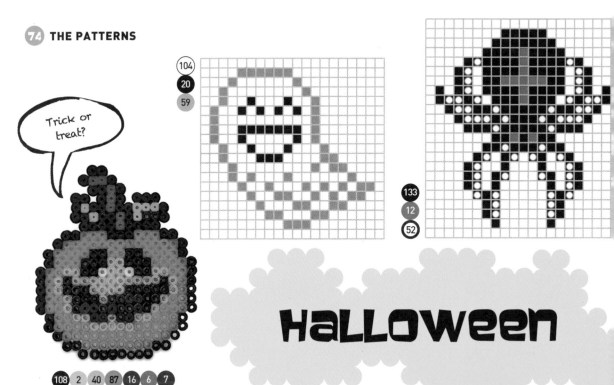

Trick or treat?

104
20
59

133
12
52

108 2 40 87 16 6 7

HALLOWEEN

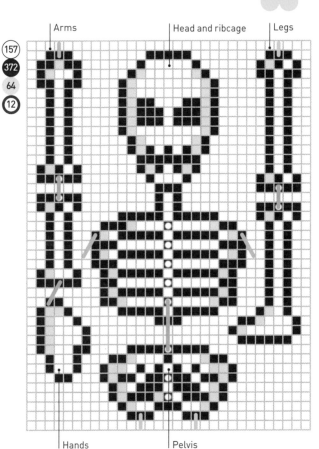

Arms | Head and ribcage | Legs

157
372
64
12

Hands | Pelvis

164 2 18

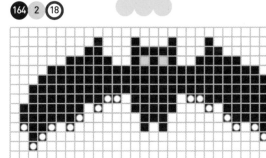

CONNECTING UP YOUR SKELETON

1. Create all the pieces visible on the chart (left). Make two sets of legs, arms, and hands.

2. Connect the head, ribcage, and pelvis together using jump rings (see page 15).

3. Connect the individual bones to create the limbs and add the hands to the arms.

4. Connect the arms to the shoulders and the legs to the pelvis.

(2) 124 8 9 5 116 41 (4)

(24)
89
81
32

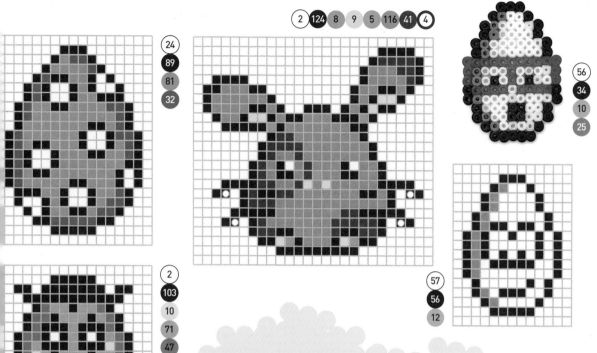

56
34
10
25

(2)
103
10
71
47

57
56
12

easteR

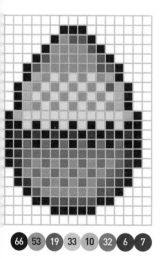

66 53 19 33 10 32 6 7

Cheep cheep...

(2)
112
16
83
44
28

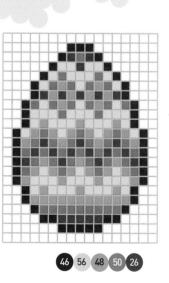

46 56 48 50 26

67
155
34
22
23
52
44

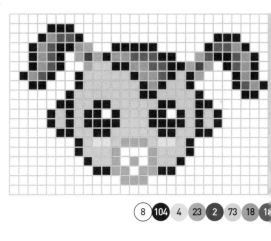

8 104 4 23 2 73 18 1

BaBY

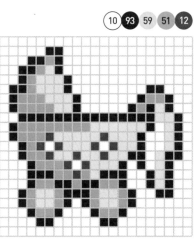

8
80
15
70
12
14

94 72 58 64 3 26 9 28 8

21 8 9 14 30 27

10 93 59 51 12

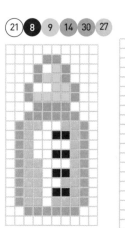

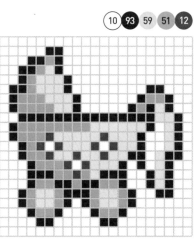

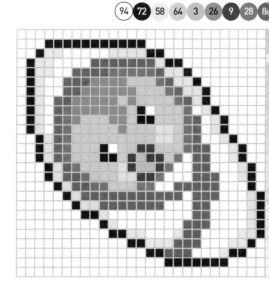

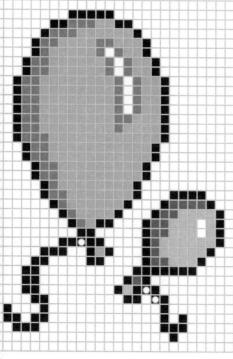

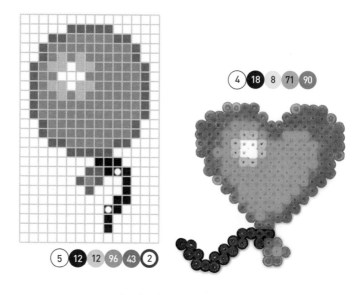

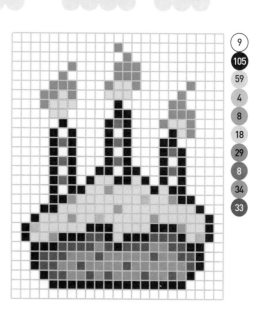

BIRTHDAY

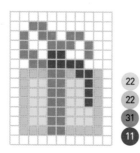

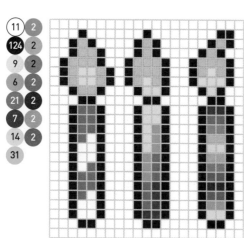

abstract

repeating patterns

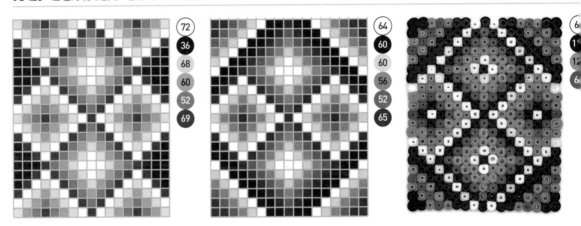

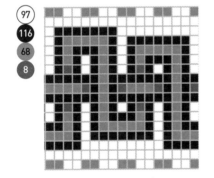

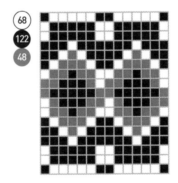

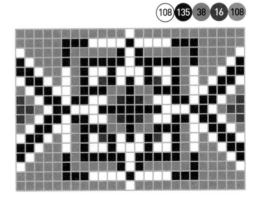

BEADWEAVING

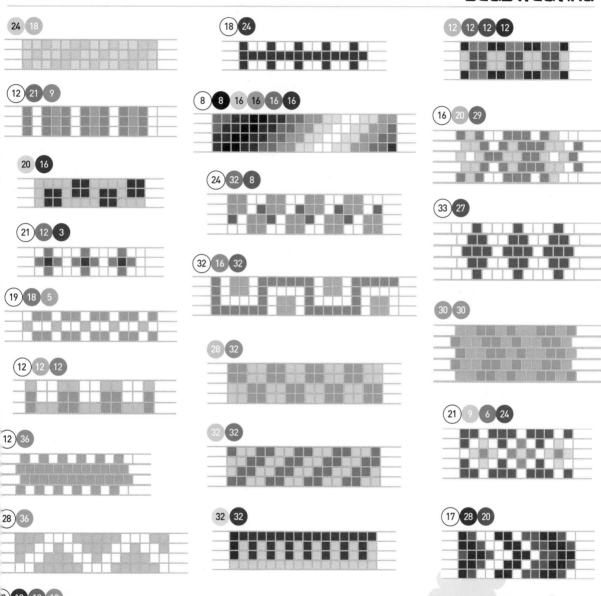

TIP! The first line of beads you thread always becomes both the first row and the second row of your design. You can lay the pattern out in front of you and add numbers to the beads before you start threading so that you don't make a mistake.

HEXAGONS

36 37 36 36 36 36

90 91 36

40 89 24 64

74 89 36 18

102 78 37

52 87 52 26

80 137

42 67 22 14 14 22 14 22

97 120

27 109 27 27 27

SQUARES

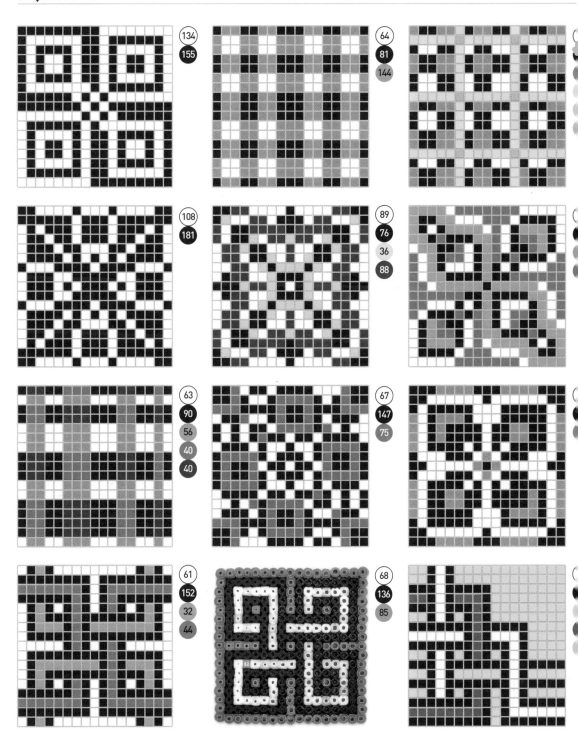

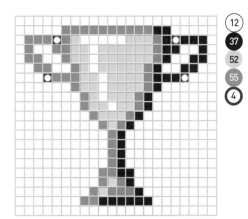

(12) (37) (52) (55) (4)

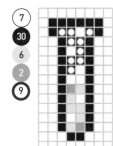

(7) (30) (6) (2) (9)

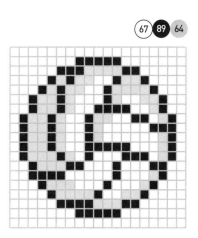

(67) (89) (64)

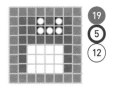

(19) (5) (12)

BACK TO SCHOOL

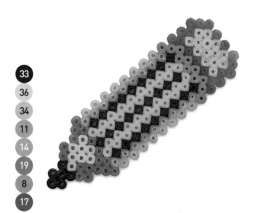

(33) (36) (34) (11) (14) (19) (8) (17)

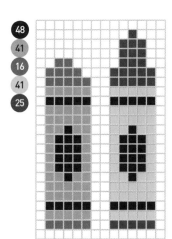

(48) (41) (16) (41) (25)

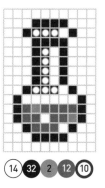

(14) (32) (2) (12) (10)

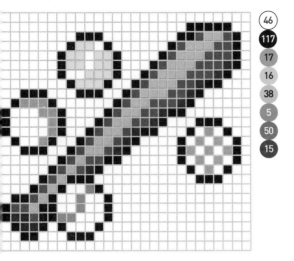

46
117
17
16
38
5
50
15

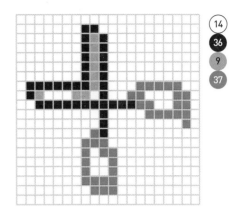

14
36
9
37

33
44
43
8

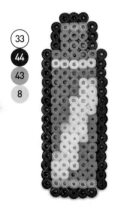

15 44 3 27 13

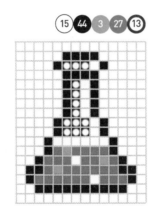

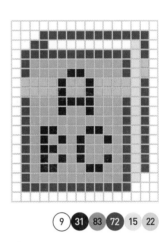

9 31 83 72 15 22

17
35
113
31
17

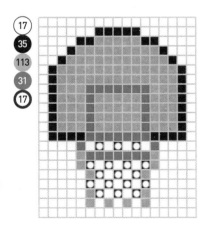

6
51
31
5
12

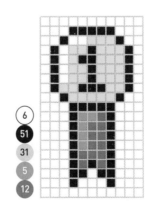

12
45
7
2
6
21
12
31

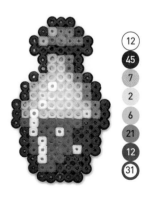

TRAVEL

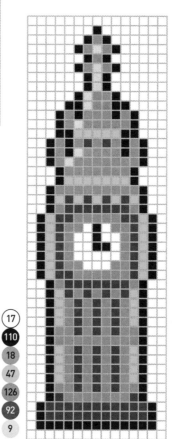

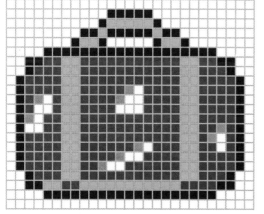

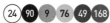

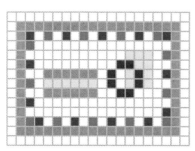

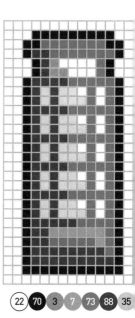

68 137 222 52 7 40 22 4 26 10

24 90 9 76 49 168

163 56 8 15 13 13

17
110
18
47
126
92
9

22 70 3 7 73 88 35

18 200 41 3 6 51 77

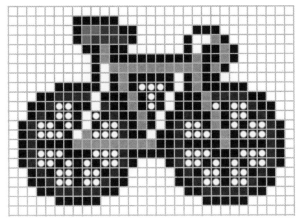

124 96 31 9 1 41 10

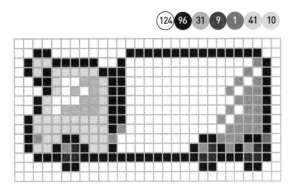

TRANSPORT

101 117 33 31 10 4

7 130 49 48 27 55 2 1 41

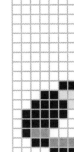

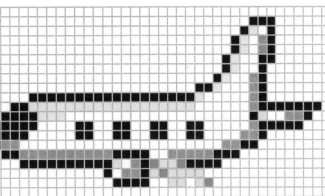

67 59 20 6 4 2 14 22

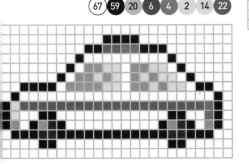

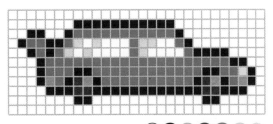

15 62 4 6 69 1 7

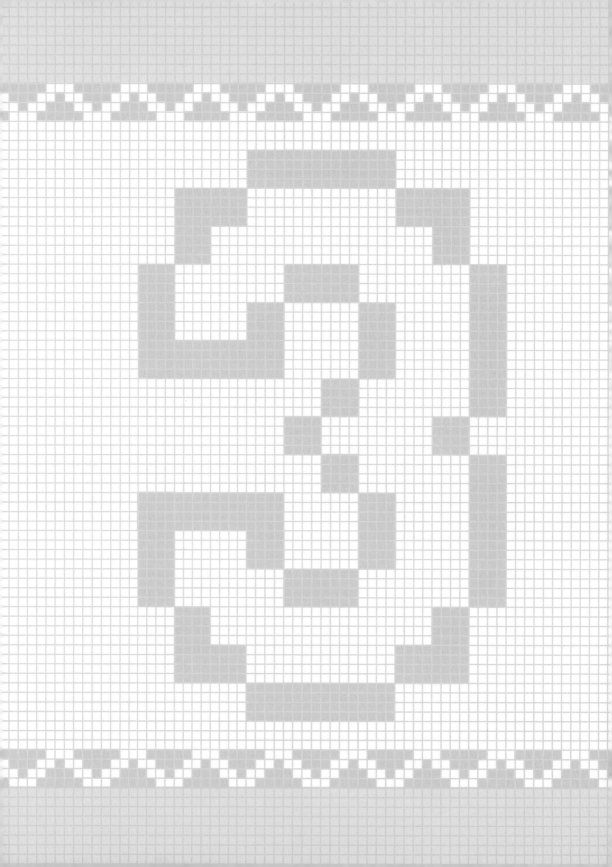

THE PROJECTS

LOVE PARROTS NECKLACE

THIS NECKLACE IS THE PERFECT GIFT TO SHOW YOUR LOVED ONE HOW MUCH YOU CARE ABOUT THEM. IT'S UNIQUE, PLAYFUL, AND DEFINITELY FOR SOMEONE WHO LOVES PARROTS!

BEADS NEEDED

20 4 28 62 21 10 20

Use 5 mm beads on a square pegboard

OTHER MATERIALS

- 20 in. (50 cm) cable chain with 2 mm to 3 mm round links
- 6 x 4 mm jump rings
- Toggle clasp
- Round-nose pliers
- Needle-nose pliers
- Wire cutters

MAKING THE NECKLACE

1 Make the two parrots and the heart shape from the chart (right).

2 Open the jump rings with pliers (see page 15). Attach one jump ring to the top of each parrot's head and two to the outer corners of the heart. Keep the loops open.

3 Loop the jump ring on the left of the heart through the first parrot's beak, then close the jump ring (see page 15), hiding the join inside the beak. Repeat on the other side of the heart.

4 Cut the chain in half. Open the two remaining jump rings. Loop one jump ring through one end of the first chain and one half of the toggle clasp, then close the jump ring. Repeat with the second jump ring, chain, and the remaining half of the clasp.

5 Loop the other ends of the chains through the jump rings that are already attached to the parrots' heads, then close the jump rings, hiding the joins inside the beads. And you're done!

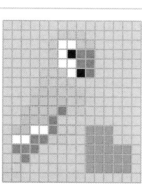

SNOWFLAKE STUD EARRINGS

THERE'S SOMETHING ABOUT THE FIRST SNOWFLAKES OF WINTER THAT BRINGS OUT THE CHILD IN EVERYONE. SO WHY NOT CREATE THESE BEAUTIFUL STUD EARRINGS TO ACCOMPANY YOU ON YOUR NEXT SNOWY ADVENTURE?

BEADS NEEDED

 19 24

Use 2.5 mm beads on a mini hexagon pegboard

OTHER MATERIALS

- Pair of flat-backed stud earrings
- Iron
- Parchment paper
- Quick-fix Super Glue or hot glue gun

MAKING THE EARRINGS

1 Make two snowflakes in your chosen design, following the chart below, working from the center in a circular motion and moving outward.

2 Iron both sides of the motif, paying special attention to the outer corners of the snowflake. This will prevent the breaking of the fragile parts of the pattern.

3 Place the snowflakes on a flat surface.

4 Apply a blob of glue to the earring backs and place them on the snowflakes.

5 Leave to dry.

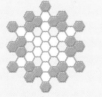

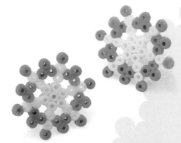

TIP! If any glue seeps through onto the front of the earring, use a tiny bit of nail polish remover to get rid of it.

CHERRY EARRINGS

THESE DELIGHTFUL CHERRY EARRINGS ARE ALMOST GOOD ENOUGH TO EAT! THEY'LL MAKE A WONDERFUL WAY TO WELCOME SUMMER INTO YOUR LIFE WITH A BRIGHT POP OF COLOR.

MAKING THE EARRINGS

1 Make two cherries, following the chart below. Construct the outline first, then fill in the middle with the appropriate colors, working from the outside inward.

2 Iron both sides of the motif, but ensure that the holes in the beads are still visible (see page 13).

3 Open a jump ring with pliers (see page 15). Loop the jump ring through both the highest point of a cherry and the loop on the bottom of an earring hook.

4 Close the jump ring (see page 15), hiding the join inside the beads.

5 Repeat steps 3 and 4 to make the second earring.

BEADS NEEDED

Use 2.5 mm beads on a mini square pegboard

OTHER MATERIALS

- 2 x 2 mm jump rings
- 2 x earring hooks
- Iron
- Parchment paper
- Flat-nose pliers
- Needle-nose pliers

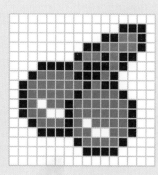

FRUITY DRINK COVERS

BEADS NEEDED

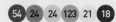 54 24 24 123 21 18

WATERMELON: use 5 mm beads on a round pegboard

 54 126 36 48

LEMON: use 5 mm beads on a round pegboard

 36 90 54 36 48

ORANGE: use 5 mm beads on a round pegboard

OTHER MATERIALS

- Iron
- Parchment paper

HERE'S HOW TO CREATE A FRUIT-THEMED COVER TO KEEP WASPS AND BUGS FROM GETTING INTO YOUR DRINKS ON THOSE SUNNY SUMMER DAYS.

MAKING THE COVERS

1 Make your chosen motifs, following the charts below. Create the outline first, then fill in the center with the appropriate colors, and begin to work outward. Be sure to leave a hole in the middle of the design; that's where the straw will go later.

2 Iron both sides to fuse the pattern together. Make sure that the beads are sticking well together and that the design can endure a little bending.

3 Leave the design to cool off under a pile of books; this will keep it even on each side.

4 And you're done! Just place the cover on top of a glass of your favorite drink, and push a drinking straw through the hole in the middle. Trust me, no bug is going to mess with you today!

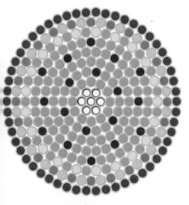
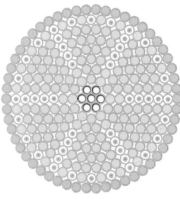
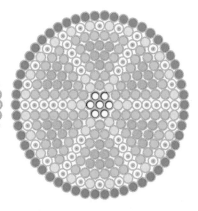

KEYCHAINS

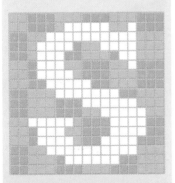

BEADS NEEDED

INITIAL: use 2.5 mm beads on a square mini pegboard (see pages 60–61 for other letters)

TARDIS: use 2.5 mm beads on a square mini pegboard

OTHER MATERIALS

- Iron
- Parchment paper
- 2 x 5 mm jump rings
- Pliers
- 1¼–1½ in. (3–4 cm) length of large-linked chain
- Keychain

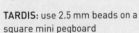

IF YOU HAVE A BAD HABIT OF LOSING YOUR KEYS, THIS PROJECT IS SURE TO HELP YOU OUT! HERE YOU'LL LEARN HOW TO CREATE A UNIQUE PIXEL-PERFECT KEYCHAIN WITH YOUR INITIALS PLUS A DOCTOR WHO–INSPIRED TARDIS PATTERN. THIS WILL KEEP YOUR KEYS SAFE AND SOUND IN YOUR OWN RETRO STYLE.

MAKING THE KEYCHAIN

1 Make your chosen motif, following the initial or Tardis charts below. Create the outline first, then fill in the center with the appropriate colors, working from top to bottom.

2 Iron both sides to fuse the pattern (see page 13).

3 Using pliers, open a jump ring (see page 15) and loop it through the corner of a letter or the center top of the Tardis pattern.

4 Loop the same jump ring through the end link of the length of chain.

5 Close the jump ring (see page 15), hiding the join inside the beads. Now your design is connected to the chain.

6 Open another jump ring and loop it through the other end of the chain and the key ring. Close the jump ring, again hiding the join inside the beads.

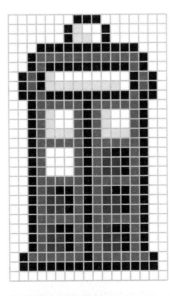

THESE ADORABLE CANDY BOBBY PINS ARE A FUN WAY OF SHOWING OFF YOUR PENCHANT FOR SWEET TREATS. THESE DELICIOUS DESIGNS CAN BE MADE USING 2.5 MM OR 5 MM BEADS, DEPENDING ON HOW BIG YOU WANT THE FINISHED PIN TO BE.

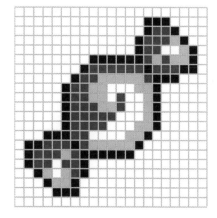

MAKING THE BOBBY PINS

1 Make your chosen motif, following the charts here. Construct the outline first, then fill in the middle with the appropriate colors, working toward the center of the design.

2 Iron both sides of the motif (see page 13).

3 Place the motif on a flat surface.

4 Apply a blob of glue to the back of the bobby pin or crocodile clip. Place the pin or clip on the back of the motif.

5 Leave to dry.

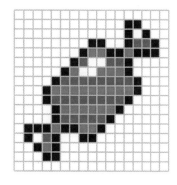

BEADS NEEDED

 18

CAKE PIN: use 2.5 mm beads on a square mini pegboard

STRIPED CANDY PIN: use 2.5 mm beads on a square mini pegboard

SWIRL CANDY PIN: use 2.5 mm beads on a square mini pegboard

OTHER MATERIALS

- Bobby pin with ⁵/₁₆ in. (8 mm) head, if using 2.5 mm beads, or crocodile clip if using 5 mm beads
- Iron
- Parchment paper
- Quick-fix Super Glue or hot glue gun

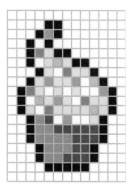

BIRTHDAY CARD

DELIGHT SOMEONE SPECIAL WITH A TRULY PERSONALIZED BIRTHDAY WISH. USING THE SAME TECHNIQUE, YOU CAN MAKE ANY OF THE DESIGNS IN THIS BOOK INTO A CARD, WHETHER IT'S AN INVITATION, A THANK YOU NOTE, OR A VALENTINE'S DAY CARD FOR YOUR LOVED ONE.

BEADS NEEDED

(11) (41) (13) (12) (4)

Use 2.5 mm beads on a mini square pegboard

OTHER MATERIALS

- Cardstock
- Colored paper (optional)
- Paper glue or Super Glue
- Pencil and ruler
- Scissors or craft knife and cutting mat

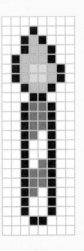

MAKING THE CANDLES

1 Make the candle following the chart below. Create the outline first, then fill in the center with the appropriate colors, working from top to bottom.

2 Iron one side only to fuse the pattern together. This will leave you with a smooth surface on one side, which will make it easier to stick the fuse-bead design onto the card.

3 Decide what size and shape you want your card to be, then cut a piece of cardstock to twice this size. Carefully fold the cardstock in half and press it to form a sharp crease.

4 If you wish, cut a background of colored paper in a tone that either matches or contrasts with your fuse-bead design. Glue it onto the front of the card.

5 Using paper glue or Super Glue, stick the fused design in place on your card and leave it to dry completely.

6 Add any finishing touches and embellishments, such as printed or stamped lettering, glitter, or ribbon decorations, to your card. Once that's done, write your birthday wishes on the inside of the card.

BOOKMARK

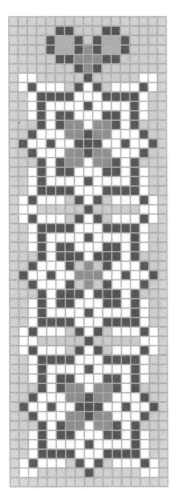

DO YOU OFTEN FIND YOURSELF LOSING YOUR PLACE IN YOUR FAVORITE NOVEL? HAVE NO FEAR—NOW YOU CAN MAKE THE PERFECT PAGE-SAVER.

MAKING THE BOOKMARK

1 Make the bookmark in your chosen design, following the charts on pages 82–83. Construct the inner outline in purple or blue first (depending on the design you've chosen), then fill in the middle with the appropriate colors, working from the center outward. Note that a lot of the abstract patterns can be repeated until they're the length you want.

2 To attach a ribbon to your bookmark, you will need to leave some room for the holes at the top of the design. A hole the size of 2 x 2 beads will be enough for the ribbon to pass through.

3 Iron both sides to fuse the pattern together, melting the beads down quite thinly so that the pattern ends up smooth on both sides, but not so thin that it loses its form.

4 If the sides end up a little messy and you'd like a more even finish, you can use the scissors to cut away the rough edges.

5 Let the design cool, then attach the satin ribbon. You can either tie a knot or leave it untied as shown in the photo.

BEADS NEEDED

   (280) (223) (297) (42)

2.5 mm beads (the exact number depends on how long and wide you want your bookmark to be) on a mini square pegboard.

OTHER MATERIALS

- Iron
- Parchment paper
- 8 in. (20 cm) satin ribbon
- Scissors

DRINKS COASTERS

IN THIS PROJECT YOU'LL LEARN HOW TO MAKE A SET OF COASTERS WITH ABSTRACT PATTERNS. YOU'LL BE ABLE TO ADMIRE ALL OF YOUR HARD WORK WHILE SIPPING A COOL DRINK ON A SUNNY DAY.

MAKING THE COASTERS

1 Make your chosen motif, following the charts to the left. Build the pattern in a circular motion working from the center outward.

2 Iron both sides (see page 13).

3 When the coaster has cooled, place it on the foam and draw around it.

4 Using sharp scissors or a craft knife and a metal ruler on a cutting mat, cut out the foam.

5 Peel off the backing paper from the adhesive side of the foam and stick the foam to the bottom of the motif.

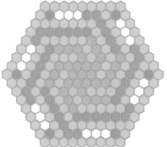

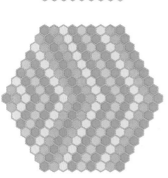

BEADS NEEDED

 56 64 33 40 24

COASTER 1: use 5 mm beads on a hexagon pegboard

 18 32 6 41 120

COASTER 2: use 5 mm beads on a hexagon pegboard

 49 87 52 26

COASTER 3: use 5 mm beads on a hexagon pegboard

OTHER MATERIALS

- Self-adhesive foam
- Iron
- Parchment paper
- Pencil
- Scissors or craft knife
- Metal ruler
- Cutting mat

BEADS NEEDED

(78) 79

SNOWFLAKE 1: use 5 mm beads on a hexagon pegboard

(72) 36

SNOWFLAKE 2: use 5 mm beads on a hexagon pegboard

(90) 30

SNOWFLAKE 3: use 5 mm beads on a hexagon pegboard

OTHER MATERIALS

- Iron
- Parchment paper
- Ribbon

THESE PARCEL TOPPERS ARE ALMOST A GIFT IN THEMSELVES! THESE SNOWFLAKES ARE PERFECT FOR ADDING TO CHRISTMAS PACKAGES, BUT YOU COULD PICK ANY MOTIF TO PERSONLIZE A PRESENT.

MAKING THE PARCEL TOPPER

1 Make your chosen motif, following the charts below. Start with white beads, working from the center outward.

2 Iron both sides of the motif (see page 13), paying special attention to the outer corners of the snowflake. This will prevent the breaking of the fragile parts of the pattern once you add the ribbon.

3 Allow the design to cool and then take a piece of ribbon and thread it through a gap in the snowflake. Use a needle if the hole is too small.

4 Tie the ribbon around your present, making sure that the snowflake is centered on the top.

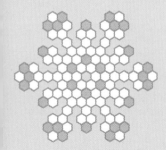

FUNKY FOX BROOCH

BEADS NEEDED

OTHER MATERIALS

- Small brooch pin with 28 mm long plate
- 2 in. (5 cm) long cable chain with 2–3 mm round links
- 2 x 4 mm jump rings
- Needle-nose pliers
- Round-nose pliers
- Quickfix Super Glue or hot glue gun

I LOVE FOXES; THEY HAVE PUFFY TAILS AND THEY'RE ORANGE, WHICH IS THE COLOR OF YOUTHFULNESS AND ENERGY! WHY WOULDN'T YOU WANT TO WEAR A FUNKY FOX BROOCH TO SHOW OFF YOUR QUIRKINESS? IF FOXES AREN'T YOUR THING, YOU COULD EASILY TURN IT INTO A CAT OR DOG PIN. COME WITH ME ON A TRIP AND LET'S GO WILD! LITERALLY!

MAKING THE BROOCH

1 Create fox head based on the chart at left. Melt one side more than the other to prevent glue from dripping through the beads when attaching the brooch pin.

2 Open jump rings using pliers: one pair to hold the jump ring, the other pair to bend the jump ring open. Attach to the fox cheeks. Keep loops open.

3 Attach first loop of the chain to the jump ring, then close with pliers. Repeat the same on the other cheek.

4 Place fox head on the table (the more melted side facing you) and put some Super Glue or hot glue on both the brooch pin and the brooch itself. Connect the two!

5 Wait until the glue has dried before you start wearing the brooch. Depending on the glue, this might take up to a day. After that, you're ready to go!

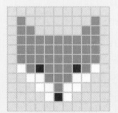

CHRISTMAS DECORATIONS

CHRISTMAS IS A GREAT TIME TO GET TOGETHER WITH FRIENDS AND FAMILY AND CREATE SOMETHING FESTIVE. THESE UNIQUE, PIXELATED CHRISTMAS DECORATIONS ARE A GREAT ACTIVITY FOR EVERYONE TO GET INVOLVED IN.

BEADS NEEDED

BAUBLE 1: use 5 mm beads on a square pegboard

BAUBLE 2: use 5 mm beads on a square pegboard

OTHER MATERIALS

- Iron
- Parchment paper
- Ribbon

MAKING THE CHRISTMAS BAUBLES

1 Make your chosen motif, following the charts below (or create your own design on pages 124–125). Construct the outline first, then fill in the middle with the appropriate colors, working from the outline toward the center.

2 Iron both sides of the motif (see page 13).

3 Measure the length of ribbon, divide it by the number of baubles on your garland, and make a mark to show you where each bauble will go.

4 Thread the first bauble onto the ribbon up to the first mark, then make a knot at the top to keep it in place.

5 Repeat for the other baubles, attaching each one at a marked point so that they're evenly spaced.

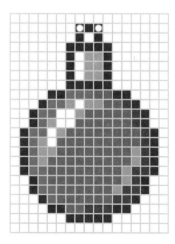

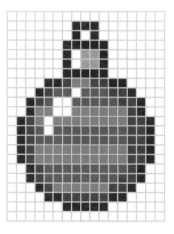

SHOE CLIPS

WE GIRLS LOVE TO BLING UP OUR SHOES— AND WHAT BETTER WAY TO SHOW OFF YOUR PERSONALITY THAN TO MAKE YOUR OWN BOW-TIE SHOE CLIPS?

MAKING THE SHOE CLIPS

1 Make two bow ties, following the chart below. Construct the outline first, then fill in the middle with the appropriate colors, working from the outside toward the center.

2 Iron both sides of the motif to fuse the pattern together (see page 13).

3 Cut two pieces of fabric, each big enough to cover the beaded motif as well as the shoe clip. I started with two pieces measuring ⅜ x ¾ in. (1 x 2 cm) and rounded off the corners.

4 Cut a small hole in the fabric so that the clip end of the shoe clip fits neatly through it. Apply glue to the top of the shoe clip, then glue the fabric on top. Leave to dry for 10 minutes.

5 Now you're ready to attach the shoe clip to your fuse-bead design. Apply glue to the top of the fabric and glue the fuse-bead design on top.

6 Following the manufacturer's instructions, allow the glue to dry completely.

BEADS NEEDED

 8   102   74   23 2

Use 2.5 mm beads on a mini square pegboard

OTHER MATERIALS

- Iron
- Parchment paper
- Small piece of fabric (leather, ultrasuede, or felt)
- Scissors
- Pair of shoe clips
- Quick-fix Super Glue or hot glue gun

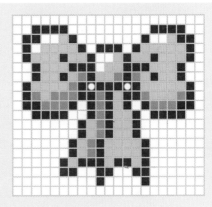

emoticon Brooches

BEADS NEEDED

  38 6 40 93

SHADES BROOCH: use 2.5 mm beads on a square pegboard

 28 5 40 104

ANGRY BROOCH: use 2.5 mm beads on a square pegboard

 14 40 123

WINKING BROOCH: use 5 mm beads on a square pegboard

OTHER MATERIALS

- Flat-backed round brooches
- Iron
- Parchment paper
- Quick-fix Super Glue or hot glue gun

WHAT BETTER WAY TO EXPRESS YOUR EMOTIONS THAN WITH A QUIRKY EMOTICON BROOCH? THEY'RE SURE TO BRING A SMILE TO ANYONE'S FACE!

MAKING THE BROOCHES

1 Make your chosen motif, following the charts below. Construct the outline first, then fill in the middle with the appropriate colors.

2 Iron both sides (see page 13).

3 Place the motif on a flat surface.

4 Apply a blob of glue to the back of the brooch and place on the back of the smiley face.

5 Leave to dry.

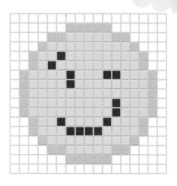

TIP! Before you glue the smiley face to the brooch, check which way you want the pin on the brooch to go

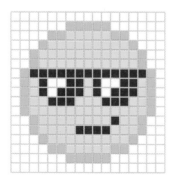

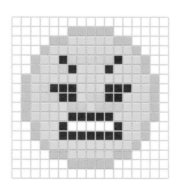

BEADWOVEN BANGLE

WHEN YOU THINK OF FUSE BEADS, USING A NEEDLE AND THREAD PROBABLY ISN'T THE FIRST THING THAT COMES TO MIND, BUT BECAUSE OF THEIR EVEN SHAPE, FUSE BEADS ARE PERFECT FOR MAKING COLORFUL BANGLES FOR SOME DAZZLING ACCESSORIES.

BEADS NEEDED

BANGLE 1: use 5 mm beads—the number depends on how long and wide you want your bracelet to be. The numbers above are based on the chart sections given below

BANGLE 2: use 5 mm beads—the number depends on how long and wide you want your bracelet to be. The numbers above are based on the chart sections given below

OTHER MATERIALS

- Scissors
- 0.02 in. (0.5 mm) nylon cord or stretch cord
- Yarn needle

MAKING THE BANGLE

1 Thread your needle with a length of nylon or stretch cord about 2 yd (2 m) long. (This should be enough to make a bracelet for a small wrist of up to 5½–6 in. (14–15 cm). Remember, you can always continue your thread in the middle of the work as well.

2 Select a design from the charts on page 79. Place your beads in little bowls or piles in front of you on a towel so that they won't roll off the table.

3 Following the instructions for either even-count or uneven-count peyote stitch (see pages 18–19), weave the beads until the bangle is long enough to loosely fit around your wrist.

4 "Zip up" (see page 19) the two ends of your bracelet and hide the ends of the cords inside the bangle.

maGneTS

BEADS NEEDED

(6) (66) 32 26

BUTTERFLY: use 5 mm beads on a square pegboard

(2) (128) 38 79 (2)

CRAB: use 2.5 mm beads on a square mini pegboard

(28) (104) 114 (154) (7)

WHALE: use 2.5 mm beads on a square mini pegboard

18 (28) 11 (44)

SNAIL: use 5 mm beads on a square pegboard

OTHER MATERIALS

- Small adhesive magnets
- Iron
- Parchment paper
- Quick-fix Super Glue or hot glue gun

MAGNETS ARE A FUN WAY TO HANG ONTO IMPORTANT MEMOS OR PICTURES—WHETHER ON YOUR FRIDGE OR IN YOUR OFFICE. IN THIS PROJECT WE'LL SHOW YOU HOW TO CREATE YOUR OWN FAVORITE MAGNETS.

MAKING THE MAGNETS

1 Make your chosen motif, following the charts on pages 44, 45, and 51. Construct the outline first, then fill in the middle with the appropriate colors, working from the outside toward the center (if it's an outlined motif) or from top to bottom if there's no specific outline to the design.

2 Iron both sides of the motif (see page 13). The side where you'll place the magnet can be a little more melted than the surface side. This will make the glue adhere more easily to the motif and prevent the glue from seeping through the design.

3 Place the motif on a flat surface.

4 Apply a blob of glue to the back of the magnet and place the magnet on the back of the motif (the side that is more melted).

5 Leave to dry for a couple of hours.

CHARM BRACELET

BEADS NEEDED

CHARM 1: use 2.5 mm beads on a mini square pegboard

CHARM 2: use 2.5 mm beads on a mini square pegboard

CHARM 3: use 2.5 mm beads on a mini square pegboard

CHARM 4: use 2.5 mm beads on a mini square pegboard

OTHER MATERIALS

- Iron
- Parchment paper
- Round-nose pliers
- Needle-nose pliers
- 8 x 5 mm jump rings
- Curb chain (measure your wrist size)
- Lobster clasp

I LOVE CHARM BRACELETS! ONE OF MY FAVORITE THINGS ABOUT THEM IS HOW THEY DANGLE AND JINGLE AS I MOVE. THEY ARE REALLY VERSATILE AS YOU CAN EASILY INTERCHANGE THE MOTIFS TO REFLECT YOUR MOOD OR MATCH YOUR OUTFIT.

MAKING THE CHARM BRACELET

1 Make your chosen motifs, following the charts below. Construct the outlines first, then fill in the centers with the appropriate colors, working from the outside toward the center.

2 Iron both sides (see page 13).

3 Open the jump ring with pliers (see page 15). Loop the jump ring through a charm and a loop of the curb chain.

4 Close the jump ring and hide the join inside the charm (see page 15).

5 Repeat steps 3 and 4 to attach the remaining charms to the chain.

6 Open the two remaining jump rings. Loop one jump ring through one end of the chain and one half of the lobster clasp, then close the jump ring. Repeat on the other end of the chain with the remaining jump ring and the second half of the clasp.

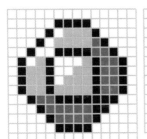
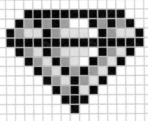
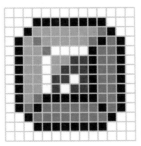
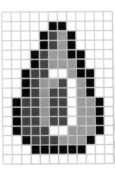

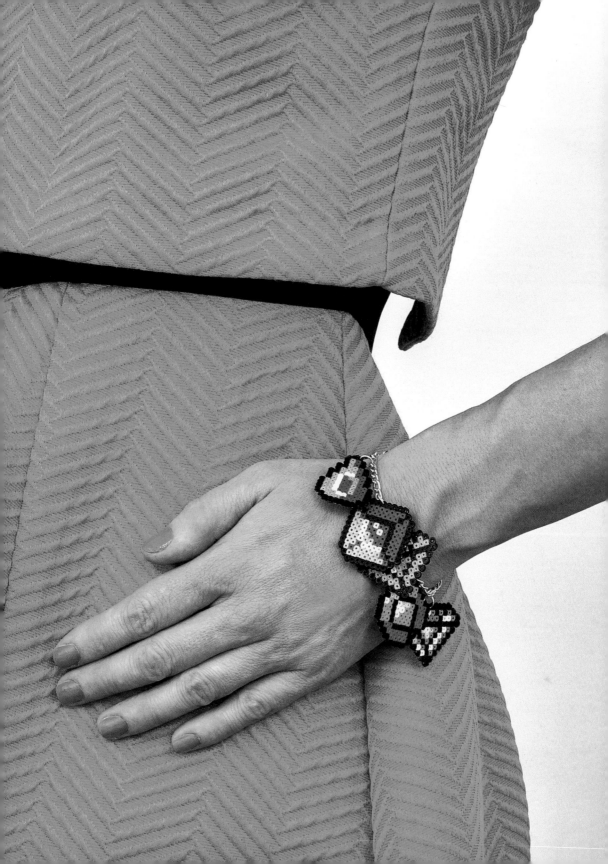

YOU CAN PHOTOCOPY
THESE SQUARE,
HEXAGONAL, AND
CIRCULAR GRIDS AND USE
THEM TO DESIGN YOUR
OWN MOTIFS. YOUR ONLY
LIMITATIONS ARE YOUR
PEGBOARD, NUMBER OF
BEADS, AND HAVING
POWER FOR AN IRON!

When you start creating your own design it is best to stick to core geometrical shapes and abstract patterns. Once you master those (e.g., start seeing your design as a combination of geometrical shapes) then it's time to move on to adding shades and fluidity to your designs.

For designs with no background it's easier to start with creating the outline. Once you have that in place, add to it with colors. Be sure to support the more intricate bits with translucent beads in corners or connecting points, otherwise your pattern might fall apart after you've melted it.

There are also transparent pegboards that can aid you. Simply print out your finished design and lay it under your pegboard, then place the corresponding beads to match the design beneath.

You can find subjects for fuse bead designs everywhere, even in old computer games. Also, feel free to build on and transform any of the patterns in this book.

Good luck and have fun!

INDEX

CREDITS

Quarto would like to thank Katie James and Shannon Russell (pages 90–91 and 108–109) for submitting their work and for their helpful contribution to the book.

All step-by-step and other images are the copyright of Quarto Publishing plc. While every effort has been made to credit contributors, Quarto would like to apologize should there have been any omissions or errors—and would be pleased to make the appropriate correction for future editions of the book.

Author's acknowledgments

First, I'd really like to thank the whole Quarto team and Kate Kirby for finding me amidst all the crafters of the world and giving me a chance to represent Estonia and the art of fusing beads in such a wonderful way. A big thank you to Chelsea Edwards for being a super understanding and reliable supporting force along the course of several months in "writing" this book, and for keeping me sane during the process. Thank you to Emma Clayton and the photographers for creating the gorgeous visuals for the book, and to all the rest of the helpful hands that were a part of the creation process.

Special thanks to my family and friends, notably Kaili and my aunt Epp, who kept me in order, indoors, and in shape when I felt uninspired or tired, who kept on asking, "How is the book going?" and who mentally slapped me if I got lazy. Here you go, I've made it now, 600 patterns and thousands of words later... a most heart-warming thank you from me to you for helping me to believe in myself and to create the best 30th birthday present ever!